*Routledge Revivals*

# From Christianity to Spiritualism

First published in 1935, *From Christianity to Spiritualism* provides a critical overview of Christian faith in relation to spirituality. It discusses themes like religion and worldview; the Bible old and new; Jesus and Paul; from Jesus to Christ; and spiritualism and values.

The author says that a great deal has been written by spiritualists about the Bible as being a book full of happenings which are evidently psychic, and which therefore provides support for the belief that spiritualism is true and valuable today as it undoubtedly was in Bible times. The tendency of critical theology has, of course, always been to diminish the miraculous or supernormal elements in the Bible, and spiritualist explanations have rendered that process easier and more thorough. This is an interesting read for students of religion.

# From Christianity to Spiritualism

C. T. Campion

First published in 1935
by George Allen & Unwin Ltd.

This edition first published in 2024 by Routledge
4 Park Square, Milton Park, Abingdon, Oxon, OX14 4RN

and by Routledge
605 Third Avenue, New York, NY 10017

*Routledge is an imprint of the Taylor & Francis Group, an informa business*

© 1935 C. T. Campion

All rights reserved. No part of this book may be reprinted or reproduced or utilised in any form or by any electronic, mechanical, or other means, now known or hereafter invented, including photocopying and recording, or in any information storage or retrieval system, without permission in writing from the publishers.

**Publisher's Note**
The publisher has gone to great lengths to ensure the quality of this reprint but points out that some imperfections in the original copies may be apparent.

**Disclaimer**
The publisher has made every effort to trace copyright holders and welcomes correspondence from those they have been unable to contact.

A Library of Congress record exists under LCCN: 36000830

ISBN: 978-1-032-86201-9 (hbk)
ISBN: 978-1-003-52180-8 (ebk)
ISBN: 978-1-032-86203-3 (pbk)

Book DOI 10.4324/9781003521808

# FROM CHRISTIANITY TO SPIRITUALISM

*by*

C. T. CAMPION, M.A.
(*Oriel College, Oxford*)

LONDON
GEORGE ALLEN & UNWIN LTD
MUSEUM STREET

FIRST PUBLISHED IN 1935

*All rights reserved*

———

Printed in Great Britain by
NEILL & CO., LTD., EDINBURGH.

# CONTENTS

| CHAPTER | | PAGE |
|---|---|---|
| | INTRODUCTION | 7 |
| I. | RELIGION AND WORLD-VIEW | 11 |
| II. | THE BIBLE—OLD AND NEW | 25 |
| III. | JESUS | 52 |
| IV. | PAUL | 78 |
| V. | FROM JESUS TO CHRIST | 94 |
| VI. | SPIRITUALISM | 108 |
| VII. | VALUES | 132 |
| | BIBLIOGRAPHY | 143 |
| | INDEX | 145 |

# INTRODUCTION

THE title of this book gives in general terms the object with which it has been written, but it will perhaps be clearer if I describe the general religious position to-day, as I conceive it. There is on the one hand, as all can recognise, an old and firmly established religion which claims the allegiance of the greater part of Europe, America, and Australia, while facing it is a world-wide movement which is partly a science and, though it is not yet an organised religion, is believed in and practised in a religious spirit. When one considers the size and influence of the whole Catholic Church, Anglican, Roman, and Eastern together with the millions of Protestants in less organised bodies, and on the other side the million or two of unorganised Spiritualists scattered over all parts of the world, one can hardly avoid comparing the combatants to Goliath and David, the latter armed merely with his sling and the stone. But these simple weapons proved in his hands quite effective, and so in good time will the stone of the Spiritualists prove. What is that stone? The doctrine of Survival, or the continuation of life beyond the grave. We all have indeed to go through the change called death, but we Spiritualists know that it is merely the stripping off of our garment of the flesh preparatory to entering another state of existence in a world far more wonderful, beautiful, and happy than this one. It is true, of course, that Christianity offers a future life, but it gives very vague information about its nature and no scientific reasons for believing in it.

There is, indeed, a superficial similarity between the two rivals, for each claims to get its information about the other world from that world itself. Christianity claims to start from a revelation which was completed and guaranteed by a divine-human person who came down from heaven for our salvation. Spiritualism gets it by observation and experiments, which are completed by innumerable messages from human inhabitants of that world. Of course there can be, and there are, conscious fraud, and also unconscious mistakes, but there is an amply sufficient number of each class of phenomena scientifically guaranteed as reliable.

A great deal has been written by Spiritualists about the Bible as being a book full of happenings which are evidently psychic, and which therefore provide support for the belief that Spiritualism is true and valuable to-day as it undoubtedly was in Bible times. Their claim is quite justified, but it must not be over-valued. *The Bible is not Christianity*, and we know now, in the light of recent critical theology, that Christianity depends upon it for evidential support to its claims much less than was believed a century ago. The tendency of critical theology has, of course, always been to diminish the miraculous or supernormal element in the Bible,

## INTRODUCTION 9

and spiritualist explanations have rendered that process easier and more thorough.

But the latest phase of criticism has only been made possible by the discovery of, and the application to New Testament criticism of the so-called Apocalyptic books (see chap. ii. p. 47; chap. iii. p. 53), most of which belong to the century before and the century after the beginning of our era. Their importance was realised about forty years ago, and the most thorough study of them and the fullest application of them to explain Christian origins has been made by Dr Albert Schweitzer. There were in Palestine in those two centuries two forms of Judaism, the Apocalyptic and the Pharisaic, which developed later into Christianity and Talmudic Judaism respectively. The Baptist, Jesus, and St Paul were the chief exponents in actual life of the former, and after studying in the light of its documents the Synoptic record of the life of Jesus, Dr Schweitzer has given us his view of that life in the second half of Chapter xix of *The Quest of the Historical Jesus*. Since then he has studied in the same light the beliefs of St Paul, and has shown how, with a foundation of some traditional beliefs, they are mostly derived from this new source of information. (*The Mysticism of Paul the Apostle*. A. & C. Black, 1931.) They are also wholly Jewish, not influenced at all by the Mystery religions, nor by Hellenistic thought, though it was St Paul who made the new creed capable of being Hellenised in the next century by Polycarp and Ignatius and the other early Christian fathers.

This book could not have been written without the help of this new interpretation of Jesus and St Paul, and its title might well have been made

FROM CHRISTIANITY TO SPIRITUALISM

(*via* Schweitzerism)

In case any readers should think that I have been too destructive in the criticism of Christianity and not sufficiently constructive as to what is to take its place, let me offer this quotation from the current issue of *Psychic News* (11, viii. 1934), and refer them to what I have written in Chapter IV, p. 93, about St Paul and the Judaisers.

"One must remember, too, that there are thousands of non-Christians inquiring into Spiritualism. It would be foolish to say to these inquirers, some of whom may be Jews, Buddhists, or Mahommedans, 'You cannot become a Spiritualist unless you also become a Christian.' The fact is that the spirit-world does not care about designations. It is not what you call yourself that counts. It is the way you live your life."

"The passport to the Kingdom of Heaven does not consist of a label. It is only gained by the living of a life in a spirit of unselfish service. Creeds, dogmas, and labels are valueless unless they inspire a man to be of greater service than he was before. 'Salvation' can only come to those who 'save' themselves."

# FROM CHRISTIANITY TO SPIRITUALISM

CHAPTER I

## RELIGION AND WORLD-VIEW

"WHILE reflecting on the current of civilisation in which we are living I was struck by the strange and inexorable connections which exist between civilisation and our view of the world as a whole." So writes Dr Schweitzer at the beginning of his Preface to *Civilisation and Ethics*, the second volume of his projected four volumes on the Philosophy of Civilisation.

He speaks of such a view of the world usually as a "world-view." What is meant by that? It means so much as we can at any given time see, and describe, of the universe within which our little globe revolves. First our little globe itself; then the universe as visible to the naked eye, with or without telescope and microscope; then what we guess as to what is in the invisible world beyond our sight, if such an invisible world is proved to exist, as all except a few men have taken for granted. This is the basis for every one who thinks and acts, but not every one thinks enough to conceive it as a rational and systematic whole. It may be no more to a peasant than a patch of sky with a god of some sort, or gods of some sort, above it, and a patch of earth beneath him upon which he eats, sleeps, and works.

There was some sort of world-view, then, held by the founder and earliest adherents of every religion that has risen to the position of a world-religion, and even by the savages whose religion does not rise above a low form of fetishism or animism. Perhaps, indeed, we had better say of all primitive men alike, that they have one unvarying background behind their patch of earth, viz. the black curtain of death, while in front of it lies a world open to exploration by science and thought. Through the progress made by those two forces that world grows slowly larger and longer lasting, and also more intelligible. The reader can please himself as to the date, or the period of pre-history, at which he considers that man acquired some correct knowledge of the world around him.

It is impossible to sketch here the world-views which have prevailed in various parts of the world, but we may take as a specimen that which, perhaps, we know best, the Greek view with its Olympian theology. That view held that the universe was divided between three brother gods, Zeus, Poseidon, and Hades, who ruled respectively the earth and air, the ocean, and the underworld. To enter this last souls had to cross the River Styx, which formed the boundary between it and the world outside. This

## RELIGION AND WORLD-VIEW

was a dismal realm, peopled by "shades," simulacra of men and women, who lived a dreary and useless half-life, of which Achilles, meeting Odysseus in Hades, says to him:

"Speak not smoothly of death, I beseech, O famous Odysseus!
Better by far to remain upon earth as the thrall of another,
E'en of a portionless man that hath means right scanty for living,
Rather than rule sole king in the realm of the bodiless phantoms."

—*Odyssey*, xi. 488 ff.

Of another world-view, the Jewish, we can form a better picture with the aid of the mythical narratives of Genesis i.–xi. The earth was held to be a solid structure, floating on the surface of the great deep. Above it was the firmament, a huge overarching vault with windows in it, which were opened to let the waters above the firmament fall to join those from the fountains of the great deep to flood the earth. Beneath the vault moved the sun, the moon, and the stars, and inside the earth was a huge space called Sheol, to which all the dead went, good and bad alike, to live just such a shadowy and unreal life as in the underworld of pagan thought.

The first application of reasoned thought was made by a Greek of the seventh century, Thales of Miletus, 625 B.C., who was the first man in history to look behind the infinite variety of nature for some single principle to which all can be reduced. "Out of what were all things made?" was his question, and "Out of water" was his answer. That was of course wrong, but we see in his question the first expression of the Greek mind with its desire to know, and its clear, rational thinking. This was the starting-point of Greek science, and indeed of all Western science. Its development we cannot sketch here. It will suffice to give three familiar names, which indicate, perhaps, the three biggest steps in the growth of human knowledge.

Ptolemy (A.D. 70) summarised the astronomical and geographical knowledge of the ancient world, and gave the world a theory of the movements of the heavenly bodies which, though incorrect, served mankind till Copernicus handled on his deathbed, in A.D. 1543, the first printed copy of his book *De Revolutionibus Orbium Celestium*. This first told the world the, to us, elementary fact that the earth revolves round the sun, and so made modern astronomy possible.

The next name that we need mention is that of the man, Charles Darwin (1809–1882), who gave the world and the human race what seemed an unimaginable extension both backwards and forwards in time by discovering and proving the truth of the theory of evolution. What extension of our world-view was still possible? First space; then time; then what? An extension into the fourth dimension; that is, into the unseen and the spiritual.

In this sphere no outstanding name can be given; but from the two Fox sisters, who in 1848 first asked an intelligent question and got an intelligent answer from the discarnate spirit who rapped on the walls of their bedroom in Hydesville (N.Y.), a continuous line of investigators, small and great, have carried on the search for truth. Perhaps the best known and the weightiest of the earlier names is that of Dr A. R. Wallace, the co-discoverer with Darwin of the theory of evolution, who wrote as long ago as 1874 in a book called *Miracles and Modern Spiritualism*: "Up to the time when I first became acquainted with the facts of Spiritualism I was a confirmed philosophical sceptic, rejoicing in the works of Voltaire, Strauss, and Carl Vogt, and an ardent admirer (as I still am) of Herbert Spencer. I was so thorough and confirmed a materialist that I could not at that time find a place in my mind for the conception of spiritual existence, or for any other agencies in the universe than matter and force. Facts, however, are stubborn things. My curiosity was first excited by some slight but inexplicable phenomena occurring in a friend's family, and my desire for knowledge and love of truth forced me to continue the inquiry."

"The facts became more and more assured, more and more varied, more and more removed from anything that modern science taught or modern philosophy speculated on. The facts beat me.

They compelled me to accept them as facts long before I could accept the spiritual explanation of them; there was at that time 'no place in my fabric of thought into which they could be fitted.' By slow degrees a place was made; but it was made, not by any preconceived or theoretical opinions, but by continuous action of fact after fact which could not be got rid of in any other way."

Again (p. 211) he writes: "My position, therefore, is that the facts of Spiritualism in their entirety do not require further confirmation. They are proved quite as well as any other facts are proved in other sciences; and it is not denial or quibbling that can disprove any of them but only fresh facts and accurate deductions from those facts."

Accepting the above for the present as the salient facts of the world-view as the latter presents itself at various epochs apart from religion, let us ask how the world-view offered by the Bible, and later by Christianity, agrees with the above.

That which we have sketched as the Jewish view continued all through the Old Testament and afterwards, till it was replaced by the apocalyptic eschatology of the last two centuries before our era. The two best-known exponents in life and action of this last belief were, strange as it may seem to some readers, Jesus and St Paul, and it became in essence the background of early Christianity. It can be traced in Christian theology down to certain popular beliefs at the present day. The germ of it may be seen in the prophecy of Nathan, David's court prophet, in 2 Sam. vii. 4–17, and in the threat of a "Day of Yahweh" (Joel ii. 11; Amos v. 18). It came to a head during the post-exilic period, especially through the invasion by Antiochus Epiphanes (168 B.C.), and the oppression which the nation suffered from the Romans, for which they consoled themselves with the belief that God would speedily intervene in their national life to give them deliverance. This hope and belief was fostered by the so-called apocalyptic writers who had taken the place of the prophets as the national teachers. The title "apocalyptic" comes from a word meaning "revelation," and was used because the chief item in the message of these writers [1] was the promise of a great kingdom that was to be revealed, under a semi-divine Ruler already existing in heaven, and known to men on earth as the Messiah. When the Kingdom and its ruler were revealed from heaven there would be a resurrection, and a judgment by the Messiah to separate those who were predestined by God to be members of the Kingdom or had shown themselves worthy of membership, whether Jews or Gentiles. Then a New spiritual Age would begin. But before the revelation of the Kingdom there would be a time of tribulation and distress known as the "birthpangs of the Messiah" (Mark xiii. 8. R.V.), caused by the powers of evil resisting the establishment of the Kingdom, till they were

[1] See for their names, etc., chap. iii. p. 54.

vanquished by its victorious ruler. Then the Messiah would be able to hand over the Kingdom to the Father, and the rule of God be established everywhere (1 Cor. xv. 23-28). There would then be no need of the material world and it would come to an end.

Such was the world-view with which the primitive church began its course, but long before the expectation of the Messiah's appearance had faded away in the second century the theology of St Paul had provided a reward for virtue other than membership of the Kingdom which had been promised but had not yet been revealed. That theology was based on his experience at his conversion, but was, of course, still essentially Jewish. The New Age had begun after all, and Jesus the Messiah had by his resurrection entered it, as the first-fruits of the elect. Others, then, by a mystical union with him could share in it, though entering it by a different way, and this life "in the Messiah" would put them in the same condition as those who were alive when the Kingdom was revealed. St Paul's mysticism, be it noted, was altogether a "Christ Mysticism."

This eschatology forms the background of our Christian faith to-day. No Christian knows, indeed, what happens to the soul between death and the Judgment; but the general belief of Protestants, at any rate, seems to be that the body and soul both lie sleeping in the ground till aroused by the last trump. Then they will rise together, awake again, and will go either to Heaven or to Hell. Protestantism, at any rate, knows of no other place to which they can go, but the Roman Church has been wise enough to invent an intermediate state which it calls Purgatory, since it exists only to purify those who are not bad enough for Hell and yet not good enough for Heaven. Modern Christians take the final portion of St Matthew xxv. to tell us what awaits the human race at the close of the world's history, but the symbolism is evidently borrowed from the apocalyptic idea of the Judgment by the Messiah, which is to precede the destruction of the physical world.

But this traditional picture of the end of the physical world is becoming less and less credible to any Christian who thinks. The world is no longer Mosaic but Darwinian, for even if we allow that something can be created out of nothing, evolution is a method more likely than creation at a given moment of time to produce a world of such infinite variety as we see around us. Miracles, too, which once provided so valuable a part of the evidence for Christianity are now objected to on moral grounds. "If by miracle we understand either the suspension or the subversion of the laws of nature, or the intervention of the First Cause in certain particular cases, I could not concede it. In this negation physical and logical reasons are secondary; the true reason—let no one be surprised —is entirely religious; miracles are immoral. The equality of all before God is one of the postulates of the religions consciousness, and the miracle, that good pleasure of God, only degrades him to the level of the capricious tyrants of the earth."

"The existing churches, making, as nearly all of them do, this notion of miracle the very essence of religion and the basis of all positive faith, involuntarily render themselves guilty of that emasculation of morality and manliness of which they so passionately complain. If God intervenes thus irregularly in the affairs of men, the latter can hardly do otherwise than seek to become courtiers who expect all things of the sovereign's favour." [1] What is counted as the greatest miracle of all, the Resurrection, is generally accepted to-day, but by Spiritualists, just because it is no longer a miracle! The deeper knowledge of the laws of nature which they have gained through Psychical Research enables them to class it with the unusual happenings called "phantasms of the dead" of which hundreds of cases have been recorded by competent observers, and which provide the clearest evidence of the central truth of Spiritualism, the survival of the human soul after death.

The latest interpretation of the story of the life of Jesus of Nazareth, as given in the Synoptic Gospels only, represents him as claiming to be the Jewish Messiah in secret; but when the time came for giving a conclusive proof that his claim was

[1] *The Life of St Francis of Assisi*, by Paul Sabatier. Appendix on the Stigmata (1908).

sound, by his appearing on the clouds of heaven at the right hand of power, the expected event did not happen. The final proof, the *experimentum crucis*, ended fatally on the cross of Calvary. Like some smaller men before him, and like many proclaimers of new truth after him, the Prophet of Nazareth was rejected by the people, who felt themselves to have been deceived, and by the ruling authorities, who felt their position and their livelihood endangered. By these prejudiced judges he was condemned as not being the Messiah, as no longer even a prophet, but as a blasphemer!

Our task to-day is first to find out what is the real historical truth about the life of Jesus; and if the traditional view is found to be no longer tenable, then to find out how it was that such a huge structure of doctrine and practice came to be built up on his name by the first two generations of believers. It is a commonplace to say that we have entered upon a new age, thanks to the inventions and improvements with which science has enriched our material life. But this has also brought inevitably a widening of our thought. Modernism is trying to effect changes in traditional Christianity so that it may become consistent with our modern thought, but it does not go far enough. Nor has science given, as yet, any but a grudging recognition to the claim of psychic science to be a legitimate and necessary addition to the already existing branches of science.

What, then, does Spiritualism, using that word

in the widest sense, tell us about a spirit world and about life beyond the grave? If there is such a spirit world, it is admittedly, as a rule, beyond the perception of the average man with his five bodily senses, and yet it must make itself known to us in some way or other by one or more of those senses. And modern Spiritualism did begin with raps that were physically audible, those heard by the Fox sisters at Hydesville in New York State in 1848. Since then there have occurred innumerable supernormal happenings, some of which Prof. Richet (a French physiologist) has used to prove the existence of what he calls a Sixth Sense, and through widely different investigations and experiments we now know that certain people have a special power, connected with their physical body, by which they can produce one or more of the many physical and mental phenomena which have led us to a recognition of the central truth and fact of Spiritualism. That truth is that there is no such thing as death, as we have interpreted it hitherto. That great change we now know to be merely the throwing off of our physical body, while our spirits, thus delivered from their earthly limitations, enter into a new and higher state of existence for which this life has been merely a period of training. "Dead, do you call me? Why, I'm more alive than I have ever been!" Such in effect has been, again and again, the reply of a discarnate spirit to those whom it has left behind.

This "psychic" power is found in various degrees in different people, and it may be latent in everybody. Those who have it in a very high degree we call mediums, and it is through them, sometimes when they are in trance, sometimes when they are perfectly normal, that spirits draw power to communicate with those still in the flesh. The spirit world is to its inhabitants as real, solid, and tangible as ours is to us, and it is fully organised with a social life which is as varied but far higher and pleasanter than ours. Every spirit begins its new life in the seventh, or astral, sphere, in which it spends a short or long time according to its character. Those who have led a good life here, that is, believing in spiritual things and practising the law of love and service, pass very soon to the first of the spiritual spheres. Those who have lived evil or useless lives here stay longer and, if impenitent, descend to the lower circles of the astral sphere, which may certainly be called a kind of hell. Its punishments, however, are all mental, never physical, and the moment that remorse brings the beginnings of penitence and a prayer for pardon the spirit begins to rise, and may soon enter the lowest spiritual sphere, where it learns what it must do to rise gradually by a life of love and service to the higher spheres.

And finally we have to destroy what is one of the great hindrances to the progress of thought—Bible worship. The Bible is the most valuable book, or rather collection of books, in the world, but its component books are not of equal value, and they certainly do not contain a revelation which is either complete or final. Its revelation has to be criticised, like all other things, and its value determined, but that must be done with sympathy and understanding, and it would have to be treated thus even if it had been—as some people seem to imagine it has been—dictated by spirits from the Beyond or even by God himself. The knowledge which enables us to treat it and use it in the right way is given us by the "Higher Criticism," of which a short account follows in the next chapter.

CHAPTER II

# THE BIBLE—OLD AND NEW

THE Bible is a book of transcending interest and value if it is used in the right way. It is, however, a great mistake to identify Christianity with it, as numbers of Protestant Christians do, and to think that anyone who knows the Bible well has thereby a sufficient knowledge of Christianity. Christianity, like many other things in the world, has become what it is by growth. It may be said correctly to have been born at Nicæa in Asia Minor, as a result of the work of the first Œcumenical Council, which was convened by the Emperor Constantine in the year A.D. 325. Moreover, to follow out the metaphor, it had a period of gestation during which the embryo gradually became ready for birth. That period was one of nearly three hundred years, and it saw many changes, big and little.

**Christianity was from the beginning an organised system of belief and practice, held and handed on by a definite body of believers living in local groups called everywhere churches. At Nicæa the beliefs were put together into a definite creed, assent to which, or at any rate to the earlier and simpler "Apostles' Creed," was the test of membership of the new community.**

From A.D. 325 onwards the community was known as the Holy Catholic Church, and was the guardian of the creeds and of the practices which made up the religious life of its members. It claimed to offer to mankind the one safe and certain way of salvation, basing its claim on the Bible, so that, as our Article VI says: "Holy Scripture containeth all things necessary to salvation, so that whatsoever is not read therein nor may be proved thereby, is not to be required of any man that it should be believed as an article of the faith, or be thought requisite or necessary to salvation." We may say that the New Testament gives the facts and principles on which Christianity is based, while the Old Testament gives the facts and principles of the earlier Jewish religion, which in its long growth of about twelve centuries prepared the way and provided the foundations for its offspring and successor, Christianity.

But the Old Testament is not primarily a religious book. It is all that survives of the national literature produced in the course of a thousand years by a single Semitic people, the Jewish inhabitants of Palestine. The religion of this people was at first of a primitive and undeveloped kind, consisting in the service of a local god, Yahweh, whom alone they worshipped, and whom they alone had the right to worship. They acknowledged, however, the real existence of the gods of their neighbours, and this stage of development, midway between polytheism (the acceptance of many gods entitled to worship) and monotheism (the acknowledgment of one God only, the God of the universe) has been given the convenient name of HENOTHEISM. One result of this state of things was the existence of extraordinarily intimate relations between the god and his worshippers, so that religion and politics (which are history in the making) became inextricably mixed together, and the prevalent moral and national ideas and ideals of the worshippers influenced very strongly in the course of time the character of the god and his worship. This fact made it easier for the noble moral teaching of the prophets, early and late, to lead the nation in a wonderful course of development upwards to the pure monotheism on which, as a foundation, Christianity began its existence.

But the Bible needs to be read intelligently, and the Old Testament even more than the New.

For the Bible is not a book, but a library.

The Old Testament contains thirty-nine books or writings, and the New Testament twenty-seven. The writing and editing of the former is spread over about 750 years, the writing of the latter over about 60. If, then, we take these writings as they stand in our Bibles, what conception do they give us of the history and religion of Israel?

### The Traditional Interpretation

First come the five Books of Moses, the Pentateuch, in which we get an account of the Creation of the world and of man, its inmate. On this follows some history of the earliest men down to the almost total destruction of the race on account of its wickedness by a flood supposed to be world-wide. Then we watch the world repeopled, and the story concentrating on the history of the earliest ancestor of the Jewish race and three generations of his family, till they are lost in Egypt. After a gap of unknown duration a marvellous leader appears among their then living descendants, who rescues them with divine help from the tyranny of Pharaoh, and makes them in forty years into an organised and disciplined nation which is able to conquer for itself a new home in Canaan. This young nation is described further as having an admirable system of civil and ecclesiastical legislation, while its worship at one central place is regulated by an organised and exclusive hereditary priesthood which teaches it the lofty monotheism of the first chapter of Genesis.

Then comes the period of the Judges when the organised nation has apparently degenerated into a loose federation of tribes or clans which is sorely harassed by its nearest neighbours, the Philistines of the southern coastal districts. Temporary relief from them is given by leaders of patriotism and valour who appear from time to time, and their religion is a primitive system of belief and ritual under the charge of an irregular and personal clergy, while here and there the head of a family is his own priest. The nation is united once more under its

THE BIBLE—OLD AND NEW 29

first king, Saul, who was chosen and anointed by Samuel, the last of the Judges, a man who was also a seer, and acted as a priest. More complete union is brought about by David and Solomon, the latter of whom built at Jerusalem what was evidently the first temple for the whole nation, which had hitherto offered its sacrifices at various "high places," such as Gibeon (1 Kings iii. 4).

But Solomon's son, Rehoboam, was as foolish as his father had been wise, and his tyranny brought about a permanent division of the nation into two kingdoms—the Southern Kingdom of Judah composed of the tribes of Judah and Benjamin, and the Northern of Israel, which comprised the other ten tribes, led by the Head of Ephraim.

During the period of the Kingdom there came forward a series of great teachers, the "prophets"; first Elijah and Elisha, then the great "writing prophets" whose books we still possess. The earliest of them are Amos and Isaiah, who may be dated from about 750 B.C. Though feeling themselves inspired by God with messages for his Chosen People, they were by no means isolated from the practical life of the nation, and denounced boldly the prevalent sins of luxury and cruelty. They preached a Yahweh who was a God of righteousness as well as a protector of the nation, and who therefore would some day punish it for its defiance of him and his laws. The punishment came, and culminated in the Exile, Israel being carried away captive to

Assyria in 722 B.C., and Judah to Babylon in 586 B.C. Those whom Cyrus, having conquered Babylon, allowed to return in 534 B.C. had learnt in captivity a lofty monotheism. The Temple was rebuilt and dedicated in 516 B.C. In 458 another body of exiles returned, led by Ezra, the Scribe, who aimed at diffusing a better knowledge of the Law of Moses; and in 445 B.C. a third body under Nehemiah, the cup-bearer to King Artaxerxes. But the next four and a half centuries of Jewish history are for the ordinary Bible reader an almost complete blank.

The thoughtful reader may well ask himself how it is that in the first chapter of Genesis we find Creation ascribed to such an exalted God of the whole universe as we worship ourselves, while in the next two chapters the Creator is an anthropomorphic deity who comes to the earth himself and makes Adam out of the soil, and when unable to find him a suitable companion among the animals, which he had created as an experiment for the purpose, gave him a wife formed from his own body.

Again, when God had brought Abraham from Mesopotamia to Canaan how could he call on him to prove his loyalty and devotion by a human sacrifice—and even of his own and only son?

Of the organisation, civil and religious, described in the four books of the Pentateuch, or of any improvement produced by it, we see no sign in the period of the Judges with its wild and barbaric virtues and vices. Indeed, we find a priest at Ramah whose sons behave so abominably that they are described as refusing to listen to their father's remonstrances "because the LORD would slay them!" (1 Sam. ii. 25). And the period ends with the appointment of a king who had a prophet to advise him and yet was capable of allowing the Gibeonites to hang up seven sons and grandsons of his predecessor to appease an offended deity and get an end put to a severe famine (2 Sam. xxi.). The same king had complained, when younger, that if he were driven into exile he would have "to serve other gods" (1 Sam. xxvi. 5-21). Was he in later life capable of writing the book known as the "Psalms of David," with its gems of thought and aspiration which can still satisfy the Christian saint of to-day?

The inconsistencies inherent in the traditional interpretation of the Old Testament would provide us with a score of questions like the above, and the moral difficulties connected with it have at all times been a great problem for Christian apologists.

Can these inconsistencies and moral difficulties be explained or removed?

Yes, they can, with the help of the "Higher Criticism," but about that the average Bible reader knows little or nothing. How should he? Tiny fragments of this "new learning" leak out here and there in sermons and Bible classes, but to know what its meaning and real value is the reader must be something of a student. What, then, is

THE HIGHER CRITICISM?

A critic is one who can distinguish or judge, and the Higher Critic is no more an enemy of Bible truth than the knife-using surgeon is an enemy of life and health. He can work satisfactorily, however, only when the "Lower Criticism" has done its work. That criticism is concerned with finding the correct text of the sacred volume by comparison of the many manuscripts which came into existence before the invention of printing.[1] There are plenty of passages the text of which is still a matter of dispute among critics, but none of them really spoil or destroy the significance of the book in which they occur, or of the Bible itself as a whole.

The Higher Criticism is concerned with the matter or substance of the books, and is first historical, weighing the evidence for events alleged to have happened. Was there really a world-wide Flood? Did the walls of Jericho actually fall flat at the blast of the trumpets? (Josh. vi. 20). Was Jerusalem saved by the miraculous destruction of the Assyrian army of Sennacherib? (2 Kings xix. 35). Was the Temple cleansed by Jesus in what we call Holy Week (Matt., Mark, Luke) or at the beginning of his ministry? (John ii.). *This historical criticism must be applied to Bible facts just as it is applied to those of Greek or Roman or English history.*

[1] The oldest manuscript of the New Testament, the Codex Vaticanus at Rome, was written in the fourth century, and there are in existence some 1500 others, some of them complete, but most of them containing only a portion, large or small, of the whole.

## THE BIBLE—OLD AND NEW

The Criticism is also literary. Supposing the text to be correct, it asks: "Was the book written by the man whose name it bears?" "Is it the work of one writer, or is it composed of pieces from various sources?" "Is it a patchwork, or a garment woven in one piece?" "What evidence do the language and the literary style supply of its origin and date?"

Last but not least important, the Criticism is moral and spiritual. "Is the subject-matter such as we can accept as inspired? How does it appeal to us when judged by genuine human feeling? by our moral consciousness to-day? by our highest ideas of God and the spiritual? by sanctified common sense when we use our God-given reason to explain the difficulties?"

What, then, are we asked to believe when the Higher Criticism has done its work?

There is beauty, we need not deny it, in the old traditional view which makes the Book one of divine history, unique in character and not to be judged by human reason; which makes the Old Testament a divine forecast of the New, strung upon a silver thread of predictions from Genesis iii. onwards concerning the coming Saviour. But there is something more important and valuable than beauty, in heavenly matters as in earthly, and that is *truth*. And it is truth that the critics are searching for.

It would no doubt give much help towards understanding the Bible if the books and the documents from which some of them are compiled could be arranged in chronological order, but that is impossible, because so much of the matter is anonymous and of quite uncertain date. If it could be done, the result would be a strange production. Serious students would gain, but there would be fewer readers who were Bible lovers for sentimental or spiritual reasons. What, then, are

## The Chief Conclusions of the Higher Criticism?

First that the Pentateuch is neither a unity in itself nor written by Moses. We may certainly continue to reckon Moses the greatest personality in Hebrew history, but we must not claim for him that he wrote the five books which are called his. That implies no slur on either Moses himself or the books. It is now similarly admitted that little more than half the book called Isaiah was written by that statesman-prophet, and the apocalyptic books which appeared in the last two centuries B.C.—*e.g.* the Book of Enoch and the Psalms of Solomon—were written by unknown men who attributed them to some well-known historical personage of a past age in order to secure greater authority for them. That was in antiquity a not uncommon procedure and was accepted as legitimate.

The first critical recognition of the Pentateuch as a compilation from various sources was given in

1754 by a French physician, Jean Astruc, who published anonymously in Brussels a small book of "Conjectures on the Original Documents which Moses seems to have employed for the composition of the Book of Genesis." He was a Catholic, though of Huguenot origin, and wrote with the object of saving the reputation of Moses from charges of carelessness and inaccuracy! He pointed out quite correctly that there seem to be two threads of narrative running through Genesis, one of which uses as the divine Name the word Elohim, a plural which means "gods," while the other uses the tetragrammaton, YHWH, or Yahweh, which is in our translation always "the LORD." Further, the reader can see for himself that in chap. i. the account of creation is more complete and more scientific in arrangement, that it teaches a lofty monotheism with a deity quite unlike the anthropomorphic, semi-human deity of chap. iii., and that the first account is written in a dignified literary style very different from that of the homely folk-tale which follows it.

We have here admirable specimens of two out of the four narratives which run through the Pentateuch. That of chap. ii. is part of a stream of tradition, handed down by word of mouth, and is known as J., because internal evidence shows it to have been current in southern Palestine, the Judean kingdom. E. is another part of the same stream, which was current in the northern (Ephraimite) kingdom.

The third, which begins with . . . (Gen. i.–ii. 3), is known as P. or P.C., *i.e.* the Priestly Code, and was written centuries later after the Exile, and completed probably not earlier than 300 B.C. Many of the extracts from it are recognisable by their initial words: "These are the generations of . . ." *e.g.* Gen. v. 1; x. 1; and xi. 10.

The fourth narrative is the Deuteronomic. The book of Deuteronomy is now accepted as being a later and fuller edition of the Book of the Law which was discovered in the Temple in the reign of Josiah (640–608 B.C.) (see 2 Kings xxii. 8), and a large part of Leviticus and Numbers consists of codes and ordinances, ecclesiastical and civil, which could not possibly have been promulgated and acted on during the wilderness period.

The Pentateuch is followed by eight (omitting Ruth) historical books which differ much in character. "Israel's national and literary history begins with the establishment of the Hebrew monarchy under Saul. Up to that time the only records of the past appear to have been disconnected popular traditions recounted beside the camp-fire, in the secret of the harem, at marriage feasts, at the local sanctuaries during the annual feasts, at the wells, or beside the city gates, wherever men and women were gathered together and the story-teller could find an audience. These early stories, many of which are found in the eight first books of the Old Testament, undoubtedly preserve a great number of significant historical facts, but they do not constitute a national history, for the oldest and most authentic stories originated before the Israelitish tribes had yet crystallised into a nation, and the narratives furnish only occasional pictures of the most important acts and actors in that great drama which unfolded later on the soil of Palestine. They represent rather the prologue to the subsequent history, since they record the movements of the nomadic ancestors of the Hebrews and the struggles of the individual tribes to secure and maintain possession of the much-contested land of Canaan. Through these varied traditions the historian is able to trace in outline at least the beginnings of Hebrew history." [1]

The most striking piece embodied in these earlier books is the Song of Deborah (Judges v.), a magnificent war-song which "reveals the tribes of Israel as a loose federation of clans, conscious of belonging to one another, but united by no central political or military organisation. Their religion is just issuing from the stage of nature-worship, and their Yahweh is a thunder-god who comes up from the south to fight for his people. It is the song of a frankly barbarous people, but there is much that is wholesome and promising in their barbarism; and the song fits in well with the stage of civilisation indicated by those old traditions of the time

[1] Prof. Kent's *Student's Old Testament*, vol. ii. p. 3 (Hodder & Stoughton, 1905).

which have come down to us in the Book of Judges." [1]

But more systematic sources of information will soon be available. "From the days of David recorders and scribes figure among the court officials. The dramatic epoch-making events of the reigns of Saul and David gave them themes well worthy of the pen of patriotic historians. The national pride and splendour and comparative peace of the reign of Solomon also afforded them the atmosphere and opportunity which undoubtedly gave rise to the earliest Hebrew historical records" [2] [*sic*].

That earlier period ends partly with the appointment of Saul as king (1 Sam. xi. 14, and xiii. 1), and completely with the accession of David (2 Sam. i.), and the history is continued to the carrying away of Israel to Assyria in 722 B.C. (2 Kings xvii.), and that of Judah to Babylon in 586 B.C. (*ibid.*, xxv.).

The Books of Chronicles are a parallel history of the kingly period, and those of Ezra and Nehemiah carry on the history to the final establishment of the restored Jewish community about 440 B.C. They are probably the concluding portion of one continuous narrative beginning with Genesis and ending with the great priestly reformation associated with

[1] Ph. Wicksteed's *Old and New Conceptions of the Old Testament*. No. 11 of the M'Quaker Trust Lectures, 1897. Published by Philip Green, Essex Street, Strand.

[2] Prof. Kent's *Student's Old Testament*, vol. ii. p. 3 (Hodder & Stoughton, 1905).

the name of Ezra. This narrative is the "Priestly Code" mentioned above.

Even the casual reader cannot but notice how P.C. from the Flood onwards is full of figures, dates, and genealogies, and later with information about the Temple and its ritual and the priesthood. "The author lived in an age when zeal for the ritual had almost completely obscured the historical perspective." This characteristic, together with its bare, unadorned, unemotional style, makes the narrative a series of annals or chronicles rather than history as we expect history to be written. The writer's aim, in fact, "was rather to record the history of Judah, conceived from the first as a sacred state centring about the Temple, with the priests, the Levites, and, in earlier times, the king and his court, as its officials. His narrative as a whole may be regarded as the *Ecclesiastical History of Judah and the Temple*." [1]

The next group of books is that of the Prophets, the four first being called the Major, the remaining twelve the Minor Prophets, for no better reason than the length of their writings. It is a pity that their books are not arranged in chronological order, for their value is not religious only; they supply indirectly much information about the national history. It is, however, not difficult to arrange and group them with approximate correctness.

[1] Kent, *ibid.*, pp. 23 and 24.

| | |
|---|---|
| The Age of Assyrian Supremacy, c. 750–686. | Amos, Hosea, Isaiah i.–xxxix., Micah. |
| The Age of Babylonian Supremacy, c. 640–570. | Nahum, Zephaniah, Jeremiah i.–xlix. and lii.; Habakkuk, Obadiah, Ezekiel i.–xxxix. |
| The Age of the Exile, c. 592–536. | Ezekiel xl.–lviii., the "Second Isaiah" xl.–lxvi., Jeremiah x. 1–16; l. and li. |
| After the Exile, c. 520 onwards. | Haggai, Zechariah, Malachi. |

The two remaining books, Joel and Jonah, are almost certainly later still, as is shown by internal and other evidence. Jonah is not a prophecy at all in any sense, but a story adapted to convey moral teaching, namely, that the heathen are not beyond the pale of Yahweh's love and care, which know no bounds of place or race.

The Book of Daniel, again, stands in a class by itself. It is neither historical nor prophetic. The first six chapters are stories, perhaps traditional, adapted to encourage patriotism and faithfulness to the God of Israel. The second part has the same purpose but carries it out by visions of the overthrow of the king of Syria, Antiochus IV, Epiphanes, who from 170–168 persecuted and massacred the Jews, trying to Hellenise them and suppress their worship. The Temple was desecrated, and his tyranny led to the revolt of the Maccabees, begun by Mattathias, the father of Judas Maccabæus.

This book is the earliest example of the "apocalyptic" literature about eschatology or "the last things," which developed during the last century before and the first after the birth of Jesus.

The books not yet mentioned, viz. Job, Psalms, Proverbs, Ecclesiastes, and the Song of Songs stand in a group by themselves, the Poetical and Wisdom Books. Job is a fine poetical discussion of the problem of evil. The Book of Psalms, attributed to David, may contain a few by him, but some of the later ones take the Temple for granted and are evidently post-exilic. Many reach a height of faith and devotion which none can believe to have characterised King David (*cp.* p. 31). The Psalms are indeed the fine flower and the fruit of the religious development shown to us in the Old Testament, a fruit which is complementary, so to say, to the teaching of the Prophets. For centuries these "forth-tellers of the will of God" had rebuked and entreated, threatened and promised, from an isolated position far above the mass of a perverse and rebellious nation. But their teaching had at least penetrated the crust, and the calamity and the discipline of the exile drove it home. So now from saints and singers, the mouthpieces of a penitent nation of worshippers, come replies to the prophetic appeals, based on the same high conceptions as theirs of God and man, of life and religion. "To what purpose is the multitude of your sacrifices unto me? I am full of the burnt-offerings of rams, and the fat of fed beasts, and I delight not in the blood of bullocks or of lambs or of he-goats. . . . Wash you, make you clean; cease to do evil; learn to do well" (Isaiah i. 11, 16). And centuries later comes the penitent reply: "Create in me a clean heart, O God; and renew a right spirit within me. Thou desirest not sacrifice, else would I give it thee. . . . The sacrifices of God are a broken spirit; a broken and a contrite heart, O God, thou wilt not despise" (Ps. li. 10, 16, 17). Devotion could rise no higher till the greatest prophet of all, the Prophet of Nazareth, came with simpler though more exacting demands on those who wished to attain to membership of the Kingdom of God.

### The New Testament

About the New Testament less information is needed, but the effect of criticism is a considerable change in our estimate of the historical authority and value of several parts of it. It may be said by way of preface that it is now recognised as containing five strata of documents.

1. The first three Gospels, called Synoptic, because they are so much alike in the general view they give of the ministry of Jesus.
2. The Acts of the Apostles.
3. The Epistles of St Paul, *i.e.* Romans, 1 and 2 Corinthians, Galatians, Philippians, 1 and 2 Thessalonians, Philemon, and probably Colossians.
4. The Pastoral Epistles (1 and 2 Timothy, and

THE BIBLE—OLD AND NEW 43

Titus) which may be Pauline, and Hebrews which is certainly not so; together with the Epistles of James, Peter, John, and Jude.

5. The Fourth Gospel and the Revelation (sometimes called the Apocalypse) may be put together as undoubtedly much later than the other books, and neither of them written by their reputed author, the Apostle John.

The former was evidently written when the Church with its ministry and sacramental system was firmly established, and, as is shown by the Prologue (i. 1–18), it was meant to pave the way for the reconciliation of Christian doctrine with Greek philosophy. The mysterious and impressive Prologue with its novel term, the "Word" or "Logos," is a fitting introduction to the most spiritual and uplifting book of devotional thought that any writer has ever bequeathed to Christian believers. But the term "Logos," though novel in this connection, was not new to the thinkers of that period. It is found as the Word or Wisdom of God by which he made the world in the Hermetic literature as early as the second or perhaps the third century B.C.[1]

The book claims to be, like the other Gospels, an historical narrative of the ministry of Jesus, but its historical value is slight.[2] The central figure is quite

[1] See Sir Flinders Petrie's *Personal Religion in Egypt before Christianity* (Harper, 1912).

[2] Two simple pieces of evidence for this statement are the cleansing of the Temple (ii. 13–22), put at the very beginning of the ministry, apparently to make clear from the first the

different from the Jesus of Nazareth of the Synoptists. Instead of that simple human figure, preaching faith in the loving Universal Father and the morality which can make men worthy of being his children and members of his coming Kingdom, this Gospel gives us an exalted Messiah or "Christ" who preaches first and foremost faith in himself as the Son of God in a higher sense than is true of any of his hearers, and, as such, the only gateway to salvation.

The Revelation is unique among the New Testament books, and belongs as a whole to the great apocalyptic movement of thought of the century before and the century after A.D. 1. While chapters i.–iii. and xxii. are no doubt purely Christian the remainder of the book embodies a considerable amount of ideas, if not of written material, from the current apocalyptic literature. The book was an attempt to explain the problems—persecution and other things—which faced the early Church, and the writer could see no other escape from the difficulties of the hour than that of a divine intervention which would mean the end of the age (*cp*. Matt. xxiv. 3, and xiii. 39, both R.V., margin). There is general agreement that the book was written during the reign of Domitian (A.D. 81–96), and the author's outlook does not go beyond the first century.

greatness of the central figure, and the frequent description of the opponents of Jesus as "the Jews," whence it may be inferred that Pharisees, Sadducees, and Scribes no longer formed such distinct classes as during the lifetime of Jesus.

The attempts to derive an outline of world-history from this book and that of Daniel, as also the attempt to find British prosperity and Empire foretold in Moses and the prophets, are simply ridiculous products of an unintelligent Bible-worship.

It must not be thought that this skeleton-like account of the origin and purpose of the Old Testament books is sufficient to enable readers to estimate their value. That depends largely on the point of view of the individual reader. To the modern thinker they are interesting as showing how the religion of a small but progressive people led them up to monotheism. The student of comparative religion observes with interest how the religious literature of Mesopotamia which obviously underlies the earliest Jewish stories was purified so as not to hinder that spiritual progress. The folk-lorist finds in them abundance of matter illustrating his account of primitive thought and practice. The Christian theologian, to whom the Old Testament is something of special value, had till two generations ago an easy task in making use of it. He found in it an inspired account of the origin and earliest history of the world and of man its tenant, who had been commissioned by its Creator to multiply his race and to use the world as its master. The account included a very simple explanation of human sinfulness, and the remedy for it was foreshadowed almost simultaneously, for to the curse pronounced upon the serpent as the cause of the wickedness was joined the earliest promise of one born of the seed of the woman, who should save mankind from the penalty of death, which was attached to it by their now offended Creator. And then the chief interest of the later books lay in the information they gave in such passages as Isaiah vii. 10–16; ix. 1–7; xi. 1–10; and liii.; of the nature and attributes of the coming Saviour.

But to-day men with quite another point of view have to pronounce on the value of the whole Bible in the light thrown upon it by modern science. Astronomers, geologists, biologists, and psychologists join in giving us a very different account of the origin of man and his dwelling-place, and though with the help of the Revised Version we have rid ourselves of Archbishop Usher's misleading marginal dates there are still readers who believe that if they allow the "six days of creation" to be interpreted as periods of indefinite length, and ignore all inconvenient talk about "monkeys," they have gone a good way towards concealing any alleged chasm between the Bible and Science. But a very little knowledge of the latter shows that the once Mosaic world is now undeniably and unalterably Darwinian, though the energy once needed for the problem of reconciliation can still find scope for activity, if it faces the much smaller problem of the entangling alliance between Religion and History. This book is a modest attempt at solving part of that problem.

## THE BIBLE—OLD AND NEW

Apologists have always based the claims of Christianity partly on the fact that it is an historical religion: its founder was a man (they say) albeit a Divine Man, and its development can be historically traced. That is true, but fresh sources of historical information are continually being discovered, and they often influence the accepted interpretation of long-accepted facts. The history of the Ægean Sea and the countries round it, for example, has been since the year 1900 carried farther back by more than a millennium, and the early history of Greece has been revolutionised. Almost equally important changes in the religion of Israel between the Exodus and the Exile have been forced upon our acceptance by Criticism, and, lastly, the scantily filled gap in the history between about 400 B.C. and our era has provided a storehouse of new information in the books of the apocalyptic writers who followed the Prophets and who may be said to have taken their place as national teachers. The gaze of these teachers was directed to "the last things," their national experience at the hands of heathen neighbours and oppressors having produced in their minds the certainty that the God whom they had worshipped so faithfully must soon intervene to save his Chosen People. This he would effect, they thought, through a Messianic Kingdom with a heavenly ruler, the Messiah, and the revelation of it would bring to an end the existing evil age and inaugurate a new spiritual one. In that age the Elect would reign in bliss for ever in the presence of their God, whom they now knew to be the Ruler of the universe.

It is only during the last fifty years that this new supply of information about the religion of the nation before, during, and after the lives of Jesus and St Paul has been effectively studied. But this study is producing a third, if a smaller, revolution in our conception of the religious soil in which the seed of a new religion was sown and germinated. The religion was a mixture of the teaching of a prophet living in a village of Galilee with that of a learned Hebrew who was a citizen of a Greek city in Asia Minor but was brought up in the straitest sect of his own religion, a Pharisee. The first of these teachers was "Jesus of Nazareth, a man approved of God by mighty works and wonders and signs which God did by him in the midst of you, even as ye yourselves know" (Acts ii. 22). The second was the Hebrew, Saul of Tarsus, better known since his death as the Christian saint, Paul. The embryonic years of this new religion were passed in the comparatively quiet field of late Greek and Roman Imperial culture, till it was officially born with a definite creed and an almost world-wide organisation under the protection of Constantine (A.D. 306–337), the first Roman Emperor to embrace it as a convert.

## Appendix on Translation

The Bible, as all know, is a translation, and can be read in English, either in the earlier Authorised Version of 1611 or in the later Revised Version of 1884. The former is the better known and the most loved, while the latter, though far from perfect, is based upon a better text and is a more correct translation. It should therefore be used whenever real study of the subject-matter is being made. But in both alike there is a particular translation which is utterly wrong and misleading.

God in the Old Testament is called by several names: Elohim (Gen. i.); Yahweh (Gen. ii. 5); Yahweh Elohim (Gen. ii. 5), and occasionally by others. These are the most familiar, and would be correctly represented in English by "God," by "Yahweh God," and "Yahweh" respectively. Why are they not so translated, but the last two always represented by "the LORD"?

The Preface to the Revised Version says (x. p. 10): "It has been thought advisable in regard to the word 'JEHOVAH' to follow the usage of the Authorised Version, and not to insert it uniformly in place of 'LORD' or 'GOD,' which, when printed in small capitals represent the words substituted by Jewish custom for the ineffable Name according to the vowel points by which it is distinguished. It will be found, therefore, that in this respect the Authorised Version has been departed from only in a few passages, in which the introduction of a proper name seemed to be required."

Dr Peake's *Commentary on the Bible* (1920, p. 172) says: "The spelling 'Jehovah' (at least as early as A.D. 1278) arose from misunderstanding the Jewish practice of placing under the four-lettered word (or tetragrammaton) Yhwh (or Jhvh) the vowels of the word Adonay (Lord), which they pronounced in place of it, out of mistaken reverence based upon Exod. xx. 7, or Lev. xxiv. 11, 16."

Why is this misleading to us? Because "the LORD" leads every English reader to think that the word means everywhere and always the Almighty Creator and Upholder of the Universe whom we worship to-day.

*But in the Old Testament it means the God whom the Israelites worshipped.*

Who or what was he?

He was called by the Israelites "Yahweh," and he was a purely tribal god, such as were also Baal and Dagon (Philistine), Chemosh (Moabite), and Moloch (Ammonite), whom the neighbouring Semitic tribes or nations worshipped. Yahweh presumably had a similar racial origin, and he may have been originally a nature god dwelling on Sinai or on Mt. Paran (Exod. xix. 20; Deut. xxxiii. 2; *cp*. p. 37 of this chapter). Israel, however, had the advantage of a series of inspired teachers, the prophets, and under their influence the national idea of god gradually developed and was purified, till by the time of their return from the exile they understood by it a God of the universe and a God of righteousness such as we worship. Their Henotheism had become a noble Monotheism.

In the New Testament there is a translation which is similarly regrettable, that of the title Christ ($\chi\rho\iota\sigma\tau\acute{o}s$). In the earlier chapters of the Acts and the earlier letters of St Paul it certainly had the Jewish meaning of the "Messiah," of which title it is the Greek translation. But several decades must have elapsed, and the expectation of the Parousia have been disappearing before it could have acquired the purely Christian meaning which we give it.

CHAPTER III

# JESUS

WHY is it so difficult to write a plain historical account of Jesus of Nazareth? We are accustomed to speak of a "life of Jesus." But that is a misnomer. We have at most some account of his childhood, of a visit to Jerusalem when he was about twelve years old, and an account of his public ministry, which probably lasted from the spring of one year to the passover of the next, possibly thirteen months.

But this material must undergo pruning by the Higher Criticism, and that compels us to give up the birth stories, the visit to Jerusalem, and, in fact, the first two chapters of Matthew and Luke. Verses 9–20 of the concluding chapter of Mark have long been condemned, and the final three verses of Matthew, with their expression of the doctrine of the Trinity, which is a late doctrinal expansion, are best taken as "a résumé of the Christian faith and the Church's mission" (Dr Peake's *Commentary*). The Fourth Gospel must also be heavily discounted as written about a generation after the Synoptic ones with a different object to theirs, and as containing comparatively little historical fact.

The central figure in the three Gospels is one which requires very skilful and tender handling, because a universal and very firmly held Christian

# JESUS

belief accepts Jesus of Nazareth as a unique figure in history, and as being infallible, impeccable, and divine. This belief grew up after his death and was finally embodied in an elaborate creed, The Nicene, which superseded the earliest one, the so-called Apostles' Creed. It was drawn up at the two first œcumenical (*i.e.* world-wide) and official councils of the Church: those at Nicæa, 325, and Constantinople, A.D. 381.

The salient fact in the narrative, except, of course, the preaching and teaching of Jesus, is the Kingdom of Heaven (or of God), the revelation of which might be expected at any moment in the early future, and with its revelation was expected a semi-divine ruler for it, named the Messiah. What was expected to happen then has been shortly described in Chap. I, pp. 4–5. Very little, however, is said in the Gospels about the Messiah himself.

Another mistake that has been made by historians of Jesus is that almost all the Lives that have been written, as indeed all the histories of the primitive Church, have (perhaps unavoidably) been written as if Christianity had grown entirely out of the dry and barren soil of orthodox and legalist Judaism, and as if there were no accessory popular beliefs, based on national hopes and aspirations, which had to be taken into account.

Fortunately for the cause of truth, if perhaps unfortunately for the historians, there have been discovered within the last fifty years many documents of an hitherto unfamiliar type, but forming certainly part of the national religious literature. They are described as eschatological because they deal with the Last Things (ἔσχατος, meaning in Greek last), and apocalyptic because they claim to "reveal" things normally hidden from human eyes and minds. They therefore show little interest in the present world, and strive to open a window by which their readers may catch a glimpse of the unseen one.

The apocalyptists were the successors of the prophets, who, besides as their first duty condemning the sins of their own people in Judea and Israel, then dealt also with the nations round them. The apocalyptists, living some four hundred years later, had a wider outlook on the world and its history, and knew more of what Palestine had suffered at the hands of Babylon, Persia, Syria, Egypt, and Rome. And this experience had produced at last a mood of pessimism and despair, for which relief seemed possible only by some miraculous intervention of God in earthly history. There must be, they thought, at last some final cataclysm with the destruction of all their enemies and oppressors, and the establishment of a divine Kingdom on earth. This hope had its roots in the books of the writing prophets and in the Book of Daniel, the most important part of which was written *c.* 165 B.C.

The chief apocalyptic books are—The Book of Enoch (between 160 and 70 B.C.); The Book of

# JESUS

Jubilees (*c.* 120 B.C.); the Psalms of Solomon (*c.* 63 B.C.); the Testaments of the Twelve Patriarchs (120–100 B.C.); the Apocalypse of Baruch (A.D. 50–90); the Apocalypse of Ezra (*c.* A.D. 100–110).[1]

It is only within this century that these sources of history have been known and studied. They provide a key by which to unlock a door and make possible a hitherto untried and unthought-of interpretation of the Gospel narrative. No one has made such a thorough, courageous, and illuminating application of the new material as Dr Schweitzer, and the results he arrives at are startling and upsetting for the holders of orthodox ideas, inasmuch as they thoroughly undermine the three fundamental doctrines of the Christian creed. But for that very reason they ought to be welcomed by believers in the Seven Principles of Spiritualism, for however close may be the superficial similarity between the current beliefs held by Spiritualists and undogmatic Christians alike, there is, if we go down to rock-bottom, undoubtedly a fundamental difference of principle between the two faiths, so that they can never fully amalgamate.

The difference is expressed quite clearly in their respective confessions, and cannot be misunderstood or ignored by anyone who will study carefully and critically the central doctrine of the Nicene Creed and the Fifth and Sixth Principles of Spiritualism.

[1] See Canon R. H. Charles's *Between the Old and the New Testaments*.

Christianity is a religion of redemption through the sacrificial death of Jesus Christ the Incarnate Son of God. Spiritualism teaches uncompromisingly, on the basis of knowledge gained from the spirit world of the laws which prevail there, that everyone must accept and work out completely the penalty of his sins. No one can by any device, religious or other, purchase immunity. Here is a direct contradiction, and it is surely not overbold to say that no one can be a 100 per cent. Christian and at the same time a 100 per cent. Spiritualist.

But before we go to the new, but true, solution of the difficulty let us see how liberal theology has tried to solve the puzzle of the life of Jesus. It has been by dropping with the help of criticism some of the less essential doctrines, and by substituting a spiritual kingdom which was to be established over men's minds and hearts in the course of centuries, for the Messianic Kingdom which, according to both the Baptist and Jesus, was to appear from heaven immediately and even in the lifetime of some of those then living (Mark ix. 1). Let me give here a summary of one of such "liberal" lives, that by Herbert Rix,[1] which was written, as we are told in an introductory note, to give "as clearly and definitely as possible a picture of the Great Life as it emerges in our day, freed from the dust and distortions of tradition." It bases itself on the

[1] *Rabbi, Messiah, Martyr*, published by Philip Green, 5 Essex Street, Strand, 1907.

scriptural narrative, as pruned by Criticism, and keeps as clear as possible of all the doctrinal prepossessions which colour practically all that is written by the orthodox about Jesus. The title of the book is *Rabbi, Messiah, Martyr*.

## A. RABBI

The account begins with a graphic description of the externals of the youthful life of Jesus as the son of a Galilean peasant, and it is thereby intended to make clear the great difference between the life of the class to which he belonged and that of the aristocratic Pharisees and Sadducees in Jerusalem, and of the Roman military chiefs.[1]

When the news of the Baptist's movement reached Nazareth, the young carpenter went to Judea to see and hear the prophet, of whose activities the account given by St Luke is fairly accurate, but Rix refused to believe that the two were in any way related, or that John recognised Jesus as the coming Messiah. The latter decided to join the movement, and spent some time in the desert meditating on it and on his own plans, but certainly putting aside any idea of raising a banner of Jewish revolt, as had been done by so many self-styled Messiahs during previous years. When he made his claim, much later, to

[1] The knowledge was gained largely on the spot, so to say, by travels in Palestine which are described in his book *Tent and Testament*.

be the Messiah, it was "in a wholly different and, indeed, in a novel way."

He determined now to work in his own way, and after taking up his abode at Capernaum and getting four young men to join him, he began a preaching tour in the synagogues and villages, but merely repeating John's message, which was quite acceptable to those whom he addressed. "He taught in their synagogues, being glorified of all" (Luke iv. 15).

During this short early period he acquired definitely the status of a Rabbi, being known as Rabbi Jehoshua Nazarieh, and now on this first tour he treated a leper and pronounced him clean. But he bade him go and show himself to the priests for confirmation of it, although custom had rendered such a visit unnecessary. Very soon afterwards, however, he transgressed the limits of convention by inviting to a meal at his house Levi the tax-gatherer and other ceremonially unclean persons, causing further shocks to orthodox society by decrying the practice of fasting and by breaking the rules about the Sabbath, both in the cornfields (Mark ii. 23) and by healing a man in the synagogue on that day (*ibid.*, 1–6). "The Respectabilities," therefore, "took counsel against him how they might destroy him," and his answer was to take to open-air preaching, to organise a following of his own, the Twelve, and so prepare for wider activities.

Soon came two rather painful incidents for him.

## JESUS

First his old teacher, the Baptist, being puzzled about him, sends a deputation to ask for some explanation of his surprising ways. Jesus sends back a soft answer, bidding John look below the surface and see what good is being done, even the poor having good tidings preached to them (Luke vii. 18-23). A little later his family hear that he is not only called a glutton and a wine-bibber, but is accused also of Sabbath-breaking, so they come to the scene of his activities to get him, if possible, to return to a sensible course of life "He must be a fanatic (they say), and beside himself!" (Mark iii. 21). Jesus, however, feels obliged to claim greater importance for his work than for the feelings of his family, and boldly says to the crowd: "Whosoever shall do the will of God, the same is my brother, and sister, and mother" (Mark iii. 31-35).

Finally, when accused by scribes of being in league with Beelzebub and casting out devils with his help, he first laughs at the idea of Satan's kingdom being divided—not denying, be it noted, that his opponents have, in this matter of exorcism, the same power as himself—and then hints that their charge is one of calling evil what is manifestly good, and therefore is really an act of blasphemy against the Spirit of God (Mark ii. 22-30).

Thus he openly breaks, for the present, with the authorities at Jerusalem.

## B. Messiah

Like every teacher in every age Jesus was partly dominated by the ideas of his time, but only in part, and in him "the emancipation from them was quite marvellous—a wonder for all time." His great object was, of course, to carry the same emancipation into the hearts and minds of his countrymen in the only possible way; that is, by taking their ideas and transforming them. The prevailing idea in their minds was that of "the coming kingdom." On this Jesus seizes, and partly by his parables and partly by private instruction to the Twelve (Mark iv. 33 f.) he tries to enlighten them. He also sends the Twelve out to announce its coming (Mark vi. 7-13; Matt. x. 5-23), with instructions which "show how much in sympathy Jesus was with many of the Essenian practices; but they do not in the least prove him to be an Essene. . . . He was, in fact, a wholly unsectarian person—in his manners an itinerant Essene, in his ideas an unorthodox Pharisee—but neither Pharisee, Sadducee, nor Essene in exclusiveness" ("Rabbi, Prophet, Messiah," p. 35).

There follows another clash with the authorities over the duty of washing and the distinction between clean and unclean foods, after which he retires for a time to the district of Tyre and Sidon; and after a visit to the Decapolis, the district east of the Sea of Galilee, he goes northwards again to Cæsarea Philippi. Here there occurs the central crisis of his life. He asks the Twelve whom the people take him to be, and then: "But whom say ye that I am?" Peter answers for them all: "Thou art the Messiah." *And he does not deny it.* The people did not think this. The Twelve did not understand it. And Jesus himself knew that the admission might only mean classing him with the fifty or more leaders of rebellion, who had claimed the Messianic office and whose names history records: Theudas, for example, and Judah of Galilee (see Acts v. 36 ff.). And all of them had led their countrymen to disaster!

So while accepting the title, he makes a quite new claim in connection with it: "You have followed many Christs, let *me* now be your Christ. Your Christ must be a patriot? I will show you a new and spiritual patriotism. He must be a revolutionist? I will teach you a new revolution based upon spiritual principles, and better than any political revolt. He must be a zealot? I will show you a new outlet for your zeal—and one which will call for all your courage, all your devotion to Israel's cause. I will be a new kind of Messiah to you—a spiritual Messiah" (p. 47).

But it would need time to educate even the Twelve "to his own poetic standpoint" (p. 49), and the opposition of the Pharisees had now become so virulent that he had to hasten his work. This (as he now plainly saw) was to convince his disciples that the true Messiah must be not only a spiritual one, but also a suffering one. So over and over again in one form or another he repeated the refrain: "The Son of Man is delivered into the hands of men, and they shall kill him." "But they understood not the saying" (Mark ix. 31 f.), and on the way to Capernaum (*ibid.*, v. 33), and as they neared Jericho (Mark x. 35-45), they talked of the kingdom and their future places in it, and Jesus had to take a little child to give them a lesson in humility, and explain to them that the way to true greatness is the service of others.

## C. Martyr

On his way to Jerusalem he lingered a little (says Rix) to allow his doctrine and especially his new Messianic claim to *filter* into the minds of the people. But after a very short stay at Jericho he approached and entered Jerusalem, riding an ass that was to be held in readiness for him, "doubtless with reference to the prophecy of Zechariah and precisely because he knew that the people would so understand it. It both claimed the Messiahship, and claimed it in just that sense in which he himself understood it" (p. 62). With his teaching of the next few days he drove the authorities to exasperation (Mark xii. 1-12), and yet he felt that he could not carry out his great reform over their heads, for though the people were on his side, as v. 12 shows, they were not strong enough for that, and his disciples were overawed by the great men of Jerusalem. Hence a deep depression settled on him, only broken by the beautiful act of the woman with the alabaster box of ointment in the house of Simon the leper (Mark xiv. 3-9). But even this he has to explain, after all, as being an anointing beforehand, not for the kingdom but for his burying.

They were, indeed, all depressed, but Judas most, since he lacked the deep reverence and affection of the others, so he "determined to make the best terms he could with the Sanhedrin and save his own skin" (p. 70). At the supper Jesus hinted at the defection which he had detected among them, but the appeal had no effect on Judas, who, as they entered the olive-yard, Gethsemane, slipped away to fetch the High Priest's guard.

The usual account of the trial is accepted, but the account of the resurrection is said to be very puzzling, and the evidence conflicting. The facts which seem certain are: (1) that the tomb was found empty, and (2) that many disciples saw apparitions of Jesus after his death. These were very numerous, and "this does at least prove how profound was the impression which he created. If we cannot be content with this, let us cherish it as that which *at least* is certain" (p. 79). "What Jesus has been to us—what he has been to the world—that, after all, is the supreme fact. He has been in the most real sense a revelation of God. You may say that he has been so by means of mere poetic fancy. But these poems, these ideals, do not spring from the air: the god-man of any age or race has always sprung from real human life, and before he was embodied in legend he moved among men as one who had himself *found God*."

"And so it was with Jesus. When we pierce through the veil of fancy and get a glimpse of the real Jesus, we do not lose, we gain: for we see one there who had indeed *found God*—one who by utter faithfulness to the inward vision had risen to that level of being at which the vain ambitions of this world fade into thin air; the maxims and customs and rigid rules of time-serving prudence are a vain lie; and in whom death itself is vanquished by the burning presence of the God within."

For comparison with what Rix says about the object with which his book was written let us notice what Prof. Burkitt says in the Preface to the *Quest for the Historical Jesus*. "Our first duty with the Gospel, as with every ancient document, is to interpret it with reference to its own time. The true view of the Gospel will be that which explains the course of events in the first century and the second century, rather than that which seems to have spiritual and imaginative value for the twentieth century." There is, therefore, one great dogmatic prepossession which we must renounce while we are examining the facts, until, at least, we see that the facts justify it. That prepossession is the traditional idea of Jesus as a Being infallible, impeccable, and divine. That *may* clash with the facts and prevent a true interpretation of them. Have, then, the facts not been examined already scores of times? Yes, but not from the latest point of view; that is, from the point of view of the new evidence provided by the apocalyptic books. This evidence and its application may be found in Chapter xix, pp. 348–395, of *The Quest*. It was found so novel and upsetting, when published in English in 1910, that it has met with years of passive hostility, as, indeed, new truth usually does. But that must not deter those who are really seeking for the truth.

There is, however, a new assumption which we must apply, for it is a second, if a less important, key to the interpretation. That, also, Dr Schweitzer discovered.

The critical writers who have applied the newly discovered eschatological ideas to the interpretation of the life have used them in connection with the preaching of Jesus only. They "represented Jesus as thinking and speaking eschatologically in some of the most important passages of his teaching, but for the rest gave as uneschatological a presentation of his life as modern historical theology had done." Why (asks Dr Schweitzer) did these writers "not also hit upon the thought of the dogmatic element in the history of Jesus? Eschatology is simply 'dogmatic history'—history as moulded by theological beliefs—which breaks in upon the natural course of history and abrogates it. Is it not even *a priori* the only conceivable view that the conduct of one who looked forward to His Messianic Parousia in the near future should be determined, not by the natural course of events, but by that expectation?" We know now that Jesus believed himself to be the Messiah-to-be. That was his "Messianic Secret," revealed only to the Twelve. But it was, no doubt, this secret conviction that enabled him to preach with an authority which the crowds recognised as extraordinary, though without attributing it to the real cause. It was this conviction which enabled him, more than once, to read a dogmatic meaning into actual events, as, for example, when he declared that the Baptist was "Elias, who was for to come" (Matt. xi. 2–15).

## The Narrative

There is no need here to give any description of the early life of Jesus at Nazareth. We may imagine him in the spring of the year A.D. 28, perhaps on his way to keep the Passover at Jerusalem, first coming into contact with the Baptist, and welcoming his message, but not having yet adopted the belief that he was the Messiah-to-be. He is baptised, and either at once, or after the Passover, goes into the wilderness to meditate. He returns with the inner conviction about his future adopted, and goes to Galilee, where he chooses his first four disciples, and at once begins preaching. Galilee, let us remember, was his native province, where he would feel much more at home than in Judea, for the population was different in character, and the religious atmosphere was much freer and less law-ridden.

And what did he preach? He told his hearers exactly the same as the Baptist! "The Kingdom of Heaven is at hand." That was the essence of the message he proclaimed, and then he began to preach. For he exhorted them all to repent in preparation for the kingdom, and he taught them with authority and not as the scribes (Matt. vii. 29).

And what did he do? He astonished everyone by casting out an evil spirit with a word, healing Peter's mother-in-law, and a leper, so that they came to him from every quarter and he was surrounded by crowds. Moreover, his teaching and further miracles created such a sensation that a number of Scribes and Pharisees came from Jerusalem to see what was happening, and charged him and his disciples with not fasting and with breaking the Sabbath. He was so successful that the crowds often prevented him from getting a meal in peace, and his relatives declared that he really must be crazy (Mark iii. 29 f.). His activity continued in the same fashion till he judged that the time must have come for the revelation of the kingdom, and then he sent out his disciples to go through Palestine, two together, to announce its immediate appearance (Matt. x. 1–23; Mark vi. 7–13).

During the absence of the Twelve there came two messengers from the Baptist, who was already in prison, asking whether Jesus was "he that should come," meaning Elias (Matt. xi. 2-15; Luke vii. 18; Mark ix. 11). Jesus gave them an evasive answer, and, when they were gone back, spoke plainly to the crowd, paying a high compliment to John, but correcting his belief. He is the greatest of all who have lived before the revelation of the kingdom, for, if they can believe it, he himself, not Jesus, is the expected Elias. The question had put Jesus in a difficulty, for he could not say that he was himself Elias when he believed himself to be the Messiah, and yet he could not disclose to John, still less to the multitude, what he believed about himself. That would have been to make known to the world his Messianic Secret.

We see here an example of how Jesus reads his Messianic belief into history. The Baptist did not think himself to be Elias, nor did the people think that he was; he had not done any of the things that Elias was expected to do. Yet Jesus makes him Elias because he expected his own manifestation as the "Son of Man," and before that happened it was necessary that an Elias should come. This Elias had already been murdered by Herod, though the death of the Forerunner was really unthinkable. The Baptist is made into Elias solely by the force of Jesus' Messianic consciousness; an instance of dogma remoulding history for its own purposes.

Soon after Herod's birthday feast and his murder of the imprisoned Baptist, the Twelve returned from their tour (Mark vi. 30), but they had no such report to give as Jesus had hoped. They had met with no opposition or persecution; the terrible things predicted in Matt. x. 24 ff. had not happened; their return created no excitement, and—the kingdom had not appeared! This was Jesus' first disappointment, and he felt it deeply. He desired to get away to solitude and to have time to think what it meant. But the crowds were still pressing upon him, and, as before, he "taught them about many things." When evening came he desired to feed them, for his heart pitied them, and he asked what food was available—five loaves and two small fishes—and with these he fed the multitude. How? If he had multiplied miraculously the amount of food there would be little modern criticism, but that explanation raises many objections. Dr Schweitzer holds that, with his mind full, as always, of his mission as Messiah-to-be and the manifestation of the kingdom, he gave to each participant a tiny portion of the food which he had blessed, and thus, though no one knew it, he made the distribution an anticipation of the Messianic meal, which he would share with believers in the New Age (*cp*. Matt. xxvi. 29). It was an "eschatological sacrament" by which the receivers were, so to say, hallowed for the later spiritual meal which the earthly one symbolised. Such was also the character of the

Last Supper for Jesus and the earliest believers (*cp.* 1 Cor. xi. 26).[1]

At last he managed to get away with his disciples to the district of Tyre and Sidon, and during their tour they came into the neighbourhood of Cæsarea Philippi, where Jesus asked the Twelve whom he was supposed to be by the people. Then whom they themselves took him to be. And the impulsive Peter replied for them all: "Thou art the Messiah." Jesus accepted the answer, but charged them to keep it a secret, and then began to enlighten them about the sufferings, death, and resurrection which, as the result of his prayers and meditation, he foresaw to be awaiting him. They were, he was sure, what the Father willed, but his human will shrank from the trial. Hence his sharp rebuke when Peter, with affectionate warmth, deprecated submission to such a fate (Mark viii. 32), for his remonstrance seemed almost a temptation which must have come from Satan himself.

[1] "The celebration as practised in early Christendom was something other than a sacramental repetition or a symbolical representation of the atoning death of Jesus. This interpretation was first given to the repetition of the last meal of Jesus with his disciples in the Catholic sacrifice of the Mass and in the Protestant celebration of the Last Supper, as a reminder of the forgiveness of sins."

"The figurative words of Jesus about bread and wine as his body and blood did not, strange as the statement may seem to us, determine for the disciples and the first believers the nature of the celebration; indeed, so far as our knowledge of primitive and early Christianity goes, those words were not repeated at the community meal in the olden time. What constituted the celebration then, was not Jesus' words of

## JESUS

But why does Jesus now for the first time speak of this sad conclusion to his activity and his life, a conclusion so different from what he must have expected when he sent out the Twelve? We must remember that, however widely the new ideas derived from the apocalyptic books were spread, and however deeply they had taken root, there was as yet no general Messianic excitement such as with an active leader might have led to a national movement, if external events had been favourable. The wave of enthusiasm found in Jesus and the Baptist the first two personalities who brought it out from books and hoped to make it an influence on national life. "They themselves set the times in motion by action, by creating eschatological facts" . . . "Jesus' purpose is to set in motion the eschatological development of history, to let loose the final woes, the confusion, and the strife from which shall issue the Parousia, and so to introduce the supra-mundane phase of the eschatological drama." That is his task

institution so called, which spoke of bread and wine as his body and blood, but the prayers of thanksgiving over the bread and wine. These gave both to the Supper of Jesus with his disciples, as also to the solemn meal of the primitive community, a meaning which pointed forward to the expected Messianic meal."

"Thus we get also an explanation of the fact that the celebration of the Supper in the earliest period is designated a "Eucharist," that is a "Thanksgiving," and that it was not celebrated once a year in the evening of Maundy Thursday, but in the early hours of every Sunday, as the resurrection day of Jesus, on which day believers looked forward to his return at the revelation of the Kingdom of God." (*My Life and Thought*, p. 48.)

for which he has authority here below. That is why he says: "Think not that I am come to send peace on the earth; I am not come to send peace, but a sword" (Matt. x. 34; *The Quest*, p. 369). In this task what was the place of the disciples? They were not to be his helpers in the work of teaching. They could not do that now, and Jesus made no effort to prepare them for so doing after his death. They are to be a little band of helpers now; and afterwards, as having been the faithful comrades of the Messiah while unrecognised, they are to sit on twelve thrones judging the twelve tribes of Israel when he is revealed as what he claims to be (Matt. xix. 28).

And what was the fate of the "Son of Man" during the last times? It seems as if at first he and the elect were all alike to undergo the suffering and persecution. They must be ready to be despised and persecuted; they must take up their cross with him; and must be willing even to lose their lives for his sake (Matt. v. 11 f.; x. 32 and 39). At the time of the mission of the Twelve, at any rate, he believed that he would not be exempt from suffering. It was part of the mystery of the Kingdom of God and of the Messiahship that he and the elect alike were to be brought low, it might be even unto death, in the final struggle against the evil world-power which would arise against them. This was the "temptation," deliverance from which is asked for in the Lord's Prayer. It would bring the risk of their being disloyal to him; hence his last words to the Baptist's messengers, "Blessed is he, whosoever shall find none occasion of stumbling in me" (Matt. xi. 6). His Messianic consciousness shines through all his preaching (Matt. vii. 21 f.; x. 32; Mark ii. 5 ff.), yet he is not recognised by anyone as the Messiah. Nor is the Baptist recognised as Elias. Why? Because he did not describe himself as such, nor did he do any miracles, and he had himself pointed forward to some one greater than himself who would baptise them with the Spirit. Joel had promised (ii. 28) an outpouring of the spirit on all flesh, and Malachi the coming of Elijah the prophet before the great and dreadful day of Yahweh (iv. 5 f.). Till these two things, therefore, had come to pass, no one looked for the advent of the Messiah, least of all in such a humble guise as that of the prophet of Nazareth.

*Note.*—It may be asked why, if Peter and the Twelve learnt at Cæsarea Philippi the truth about the "Messianic secret" of Jesus, it is told to Peter, James, and John only as a not yet revealed secret, at the Transfiguration (Mark xxix.).

Dr Schweitzer asks for one great alteration in the text in addition to those universally accepted, such as the Birth stories in Matt. and Luke. Taking the feedings of the 5000 and the 4000 to be obviously doublets, *i.e.* two accounts of the same event, and other smaller points in the text, he would transfer the passage viii. 34 to ix. 29 to follow the end of chapter vi. of Mark. On that would follow chapter vii. 1 to viii. 33, and from ix. 30

there would be no change from what is accepted in the ordinary text. This would bring the narrative of the Transfiguration before the visit to Cæsarea Philippi, and his "Messianic secret" would have been made known to the three before he later asked the question of the Twelve. In that case it would be because he had learnt the truth at the Transfiguration, but had forgotten the injunction to keep it a secret, that Peter blurted out his answer on the later occasion. He thus unfortunately made the truth known to all the Twelve, Judas included, who made such treacherous use of it later.

The disclosure of his secret to the Twelve at Cæsarea Philippi is a dividing line between the two periods of Jesus' activity. In the first period he thought of himself as undergoing with all believers the general sufferings which formed part of the "Mystery of the Kingdom of God." So the announcement of suffering for himself personally, made after the conversation at Cæsarea—or after the Transfiguration, if that happened first—was not something altogether new, though the form it took was new. During his retirement in the north Jesus must often have meditated on the "Suffering Servant of Yahweh," in Isaiah lii. and liii., and then a new conviction dawned on him. Why had the expected manifestation not come about, neither during the tour of the twelve nor after it, nor yet a little later, when he had consecrated the multitude by a foretaste of the Messianic feast? The delay surely meant that something necessary had been omitted, for until the time of tribulation had come (the birth-pangs of the Messiah, Mark xiii. 8, A.V., marg.), the revelation of the kingdom and of himself as the Son of Man, the Messiah, were impossible. He had taught his followers to pray for the coming of the kingdom, and at the same time for deliverance from the "temptation." God had been merciful; he had not sent the tribulations, but had left him to accomplish in his own person what was still necessary. He, as the ruler of the members of the kingdom in the future Age, was surely appointed to serve them in the present Age; to give his life for them, the many (Mark x. 45), and to make by his own death the atonement for all their sins and insufficient repentance, which otherwise they would have to make by undergoing the sufferings of the tribulation (Mark xiii. 24). His death alone could at last compel the revelation of the kingdom.

Towards the Passover, then, Jesus sets out for Jerusalem, not for the Festival but for the Sacrifice of himself—in order that the Kingdom might come. From one point of view the sacrifice is an act of pity and compassion for those who would have had to suffer, and perhaps might not have stood the test; from another it is an instance of his dogmatic interpretation of history, like that of his identification of the Baptist with Elias. He identifies his own condemnation and execution with the predicted Messianic tribulation, but it will fall on him only, not on them: he will give his life as "a ransom for many" (Mark x. 45), *i.e.* for the Messianic believers, not for all mankind, as it has generally, but loosely and wrongly, been taken to mean in the past.

On his arrival at the city, accompanied by the crowd of pilgrims, he receives an enthusiastic ovation, and is greeted by all as the Prophet of Nazareth: "Blessed is he that cometh in the name of the Lord." That he enters riding on an ass is his own arrangement that the prophecy of Zech. ix. 9 might be fulfilled, and the entry is Messianic to him but not to the crowds. During the week, supported by the enthusiasm of the crowd, he cleanses the Temple of the money-changers and denounces in scathing and provocative terms the Pharisees and the Sadducees. On the Thursday evening, knowing that the end must be near, he withdraws to Gethsemane, taking with him the sons of Zebedee, who had declared themselves able to drink his cup and to be baptised with his baptism (Mark x. 38 f.), and Peter, who had sworn that he would go even to death with him (Mark xiv. 30 f.). There all pray together, and he adjures them to pray specially that they may not have to share the temptation, since even if the spirit is willing, the flesh is weak. He himself, too, prays for escape, if it is possible, for the will of his Father is, after all, above the eschatological necessity; he prays even while the band that will arrest him is already on its way.

At the trial no evidence can be brought which is sufficient, till at last the High Priest asks a question

# JESUS

which discloses that he is aware of something that was known to Jesus and the Twelve only. He asks him "Art thou the Messiah, the Son of the Blessed?" Jesus admits it, defiantly, and answers: "I am; and ye shall see the Son of Man sitting at the right hand of power, and coming on the clouds of heaven." Then came that terrible shout from the crowd: "Crucify him!" "He, the Messiah? Blasphemy! Blasphemy! Crucify him!" What had made this shout possible? The treachery of Judas. The question of his motive has been discussed *ad nauseam*. No one has ever guessed that the real question was "What did the traitor reveal?" It was the Messianic Secret! And Jesus admitted it. The evidence now sufficed, and before the evening of the 14th of the month Nisan, the day on which the Paschal Lamb was eaten, the earthly life of Jesus ended.

CHAPTER IV

# PAUL

JESUS died upon the Cross. Then some forty hours later there happened what has been described as "the most certain fact of history," concerning which F. W. H. Myers wrote: "I predict that, in consequence of the new evidence, all reasonable men, a century hence, will believe the Resurrection of Christ, whereas, in default of the new evidence, no reasonable men, a century hence, would have believed it. The ground of this forecast is plain enough. Our ever-growing recognition of the continuity, the uniformity, of cosmic law has gradually made of the uniqueness of any incident its inevitable refutation. Ever more clearly must our age of science realise that any relation between a material and a spiritual world cannot be an ethical or emotional relation alone; that it must needs be a great structural fact of the universe. . . . And especially as to that central claim, of the soul's life manifested after the body's death, it is plain that this can less and less be supported by remote tradition alone; that it must more and more be tested by modern experience and inquiry." (*Human Personality*. Abridged edition, p. 351.) The Resurrection, then, is not a unique event, but only one link in a long chain of evidence which proves that every human being is a spirit, who on leaving the fleshly body begins a new spiritual existence. So the miracle, as it was once thought to be, of the Resurrection is believed in by Spiritualists just because it was not a miracle!

What did it prove? It proved at least that Jesus was alive in the spiritual world. That fact, of which some believers had ocular evidence—the phenomena of the Day of Pentecost; the preaching of Peter and John with their bold defiance of the order to be silent (Acts iv. 1–31); the speech and martyrdom of Stephen (Acts vii.); and the vigorous work of Philip (Acts viii.)—created the nucleus of a body of believers which had to face much opposition.

Foremost among the persecutors was Saul, who procured authority to arrest all followers of "the Way," but as he travelled to Damascus to do so he was himself arrested, for when approaching the city he saw a supernormal light, and heard a voice saying to him: "Saul, Saul, why persecutest thou me?" The bright light caused temporary blindness from which he was delivered by Ananias a few days later in the city, and as a result of the experience of these few days the whole course of his life was changed. Saul the Persecutor became all at once Paul the Missionary, and the new convert with his clear and independent thinking did more than anyone to shape the beliefs of the young society.

Let us consider his conversion in the light of modern psychology, and we shall see that it was not so miraculous as it seemed to be. What is conversion? and to what was St Paul's due?

Conversion is a change, mental and moral, from a state of unrest, doubt, pessimism, or despair arising from various causes, to a state of rest, satisfaction, and happiness, in which the "divided self" emerges into the smooth waters of inner unity and peace. It is a psychological process which may take place with any sort of mental material, and need not necessarily assume the religious form.[1]

Was this the state of mind in which St Paul was? Yes, he was in a state of mental unrest; he had misgivings as to whether after all he was right, and he was deeply troubled by them. He may well have been impressed by the boldness shown by the Apostles in their preaching, and he was present at the martyrdom of Stephen (Acts vii. 54–60; xxii. 20). He therefore knew about Stephen's vision of Jesus in glory; he knew of his cry of resignation; he may have heard his prayer for his murderers. He may, too, have been struck by the same unresisting attitude of the men and women whom he arrested in their own homes and sent to prison. He may well have begun to think that his present course was wrong, that he would have to take another, and he shrank from that admission of failure. What else can be the meaning of "It is hard for thee to kick against the goad!" For the strokes of the goad were metaphorical, and were really pricks of conscience. He

[1] Wm. James's *Varieties of Religious Experience*, chap. viii. p. 125.

was ready unconsciously, and the voice of Jesus was the last straw. It did its work of altering the balance, and the new course became clear. Paul had strength of mind, too, to recognise it, with resolution enough to follow it. The moral impulse and the obvious first step was to stop this persecution and to join the heretics in their search for truth. The voice was, however, no guarantee that his further interpretation was correct.

What, then, were the conclusions to which he could come? First, this appearance proved that Jesus of Nazareth was still alive in the spirit world after his so-called death. Secondly, it made him sure that Jesus was not the blasphemer he had been judged to be, and he concluded, rightly or wrongly, that he was what he had in life claimed to be. That was, of course, the Jewish Messiah, but, equally of course, not the Christian Christ.

So in a few days, when he had regained his sight and had been baptised, Saul the Persecutor began his new life as Paul the Missionary, and by such vigorous and successful preaching that his life was in danger at Damascus. So in order to let him escape from his fanatical enemies his friends let him down over the city wall by night. He went to Jerusalem where Barnabas made him known to Apostles, but again he had to escape, and he sought safety in his native town, Tarsus.

Our concern, however, is not with his active life but with the doctrine which he preached during his wonderful missionary journeys. But before anything is said about his new theology we must name some chief points of his old theology, part of which was, of course, too fundamental to need changing.

First of all and most fundamental came his acceptance, as a Jew, of the Old Testament as his great religious book, and as the casket containing something more precious still.

"You cannot take too strictly the word 'divine' as applied to the Law. And what does divine imply? It implies that just as God Himself is perfectly just and good, so is all His Law. Not this injunction or that, but all injunctions, not the moral Law only and not the ritual laws, but all the laws, both moral and ritual, all, without exception, are good and perfect and divine.

"Nowhere is the faintest indication given in the Law that any prophet or teacher shall come who shall have the power or authority to criticise, or subvert, or to alter any single injunction in the Law. The last word of prophecy was: 'Remember ye the law of Moses, my servant' (Malachi iv. 4). Such, then, was the universal belief—be it wise, be it foolish, be it strange, be it simple—about the Law.

"Next, remember that this divine Law was regarded as a great glory and distinction. It constituted the nation's pride—its holiest and greatest possession. For the Law the people were ever ready to die, and for the Law in their thousands they have died." [1]

The essence of Judaism being, then, devotion to a divinely given Law, it follows that the way of salvation was primarily the way of obedience instead of the way of growth. The Law came in to intensify men's consciousness of sin (Rom. vii. 13) and as a preparatory discipline (Gal. iii. 23–26), though there was an allegorising, spiritualising method of interpretation used by the Rabbis (see Gal. iv. 21–31) by which a higher meaning was given to what seemed lower, and the plain literal, historical meaning was explained away. But Paul's ideas had changed fundamentally after his conversion, and he can now see in legalism not a permanent form of religion but a stage in its growth. For, as he explains to the Galatians, a covenant has been made with Abraham as a reward of his faith, and that covenant, he says, cannot be annulled by a law given 400 years later (Gal. iii. 16–22). Abraham, therefore, was not hemmed in by legal sanctions; he was able to cast himself confidently on the promises of God and to show thereby that legalism was, as St Paul maintained, only a temporary phase of religion (Rom. v. 20).

Let us recall now that while the "Judaising party" (as they are sometimes called) insisted on Gentile converts submitting to circumcision and becoming

[1] C. G. Montefiore's *The Religious Teaching of Jesus*, chap. ii.; *Jesus as Prophet*, p. 25 f. (1910).

Jews whereby they were under the same obligations to keep the Law as Jews were, St Paul opposes them. Why? Because the Messianic eschatology is universalistic; that is, all Gentiles who accept belief in Jesus as Messiah, and prepare for his Parousia or Second Coming by repentance and sanctification can enter the Messianic Kingdom at death, since by the death of Jesus the New Age has begun, and he has been the first person to enter it. But the forces of death and resurrection are at work in the new convert in virtue of his baptism into the Messiah (Rom. vi. 3), so that he is no longer a natural man except in outward appearance. Converts are already in mystical union with the Messiah; that is, are "in Christ," and must not allow themselves to be made subject to the Law, for they will renounce thereby their hopes of salvation which rest on faith in the Messiah; that is, in Christ (Gal. v. 2–5).

Here, then, is a new conception of the Messiah and his work. He is no longer the Messiah whose figure has been built up on passages from the prophets which looked forward to a great time of peace and prosperity for Jerusalem. The Exile produced a figure who would be the champion of the nation and would fulfil the many promises made to Judah and David which had not been fulfilled yet. Now, they thought, fulfilment would come, and either through a great victorious monarch of David's line, or through a supernatural being already existent in heaven, who would show himself in their history as Ruler and Judge and as a Prince of Peace. Anyhow by these hopes, which were emphasised by the apocalyptic books, the nation was brought to a universal state of expectancy which was coming to a head while Jesus was growing to manhood, and found definite expression in the announcement of the Baptist: "Repent ye, for the kingdom of Heaven is at hand!" (Matt. iii. 2), which was repeated as his own by Jesus.

All the teaching and preaching of Jesus was devoted, as has been already explained, to preparing the people for the revelation of the Kingdom, and its immediate appearance, with himself as the Messiah, was confidently promised as Jesus stood before the High Priest. Although the revelation did not come about with his Resurrection "on the third day," the expectation of it and of a Second Coming in the immediate future of Jesus the Messiah took firm possession of the minds of the Twelve and of all those who were converted by their preaching.

To this belief Saul the persecutor was converted in spite of himself, and then in Damascus he preached and proved that Jesus was indeed the Messiah. But what did that statement mean to him? Its first and obvious meaning was that Jesus was what he had claimed to be, viz. the national Messiah, or in the language of Greek-speaking converts "the Christ." That claim must have been familiar to St Paul, for it was the chief ground of the condemnation and crucifixion. But most of what he knew about the life and work of Jesus he must have learnt gradually from the groups of Christians at the various places which he visited. There was for him no other means of learning. We can read in St Paul's address at Antioch in Pisidia (Acts xiii.) the then accepted story of the Messiah and how the idea grew in the course of history. It tells of centuries of preparation beforehand for the mission and work of the Messiah, who was the centre and pivot of all St Paul's theology. That work was, as we can read in two of his earliest epistles, to enable us "to obtain salvation through Our Lord Jesus, the Messiah" (1 Thess. v. 10), "who gave himself for our sins that he might deliver us out of this present evil world according to the will of our God and Father" (Gal. i. 4).

Let us consider first his central doctrine, which with a few comments and additions will give a sufficient account of his theology. The doctrine is, of course, the Redemption of Man, and intrinsically it is very simple. The Redeemer is the expected Messiah, who leaves the home where he has been pre-existent with God his Father, and becomes a man like us that we may become sons of God. He thereby enters the dominion of sin in which the human race is living and is overcome by the death to which every man in that dominion is liable. But the Redeemer is not a mere man, and he overcomes the human penalty by his Resurrection, so that we men, who languished in the bonds of sin, are thereby freed from it. The Redeemer then returns to his heavenly home, exalted to still further glory with his Father who had sent him (Phil. ii. 5–11).

Redemption in the letters and speeches of St Paul is a cosmic transaction begun by the Father, a drama in which the Messiah is the protagonist, the incidents playing themselves out on him alone, while mankind is the mass of silent spectators who, though in their ignorance they are unaware of the fact, will ultimately be the direct beneficiaries. St Paul is the only spectator who understands, and he is keenly eager to make every man and woman share his feelings of triumphant joy at what has been done and his expectant longing for what is to follow in the future. For these are the feelings aroused in him by the fatherly affection of God and the self-denying love of the Messiah, "who loved me and gave himself for me" (Gal. ii. 20).

And what sort of beings are those he came to save? Children of God, indeed potentially, but also children of Adam. Spirits, therefore, but also men and women of flesh and blood. The flesh is indeed only the external material part of man, his bodily self, but this implies sin, for sin originated in the flesh, dwells in it, clings indissolubly to it. Yes, man through his bodily existence in the flesh is subject from birth to the power of sin, and to make his servitudes worse, the Law comes, stimulating it and giving man a knowledge of it, so that he is conscious of how forlorn and miserable is his state. Then lastly, drawn in the train of the Law, comes death, after which there is no real life more but only a dismal, ghostly life in Sheol, and man can only exclaim: "O wretched man that I am! who will deliver me from this body of death?" (Rom. vii. 24). No star shines upon the darkness. Jew and Gentile alike are lost.

While this state of things continues there can be no redemption; to be redeemed man must rise out of the sphere of sin into that of righteousness; out of the dominion of evil forces into the dominion of God. Two experiences of one single being bring in the needed change for all mankind. That being is the Messiah, the Son of God, who becomes man. "Him who (in his heavenly existence) knew no sin, God made to be (by his becoming man) sin for us" (2 Cor. v. 21). This we may perhaps explain by saying that the Redeemer takes on himself a general objective sinfulness, incidental to human nature, as it exists prior to reaching the point of actual transgression. For St Paul has not as yet, at any rate, reached any clear definition of what this divine-human being, this God-man really is, beyond the essential fact that he is the Redeemer. As such he is subject to death and he undergoes it. But again, being what he is, he cannot be held by it, and he shows himself to be alive. For to him death is not really death but, thanks to his resurrection which follows it, it is the entrance into a new and spiritual existence.

And both these experiences man goes through with him. Believers first, for "so many as were baptised into Jesus, the Messiah, were baptised into his death" (Rom. vi. 3). They have died to sin, and to the Law, and to the world (Rom. vi. 3–11; vii. 4–6; Gal. ii. 19; vi. 14), and are risen with the Messiah (Rom. vi. 8–11; 1 Cor. xv. 20–22) though the actual realisation of this change is in the future. "The life which I live now in the flesh I live in faith, the faith which is in the Son of God who loved me and gave himself for me" (Gal. ii. 20). St Paul is still in the flesh and so are all his converts. But in all true believers there is a power which will enable the remainder of their earthly life to be true and faithful, although while it lasts they are liable to sin (Rom. vi. 11; vii. 9–17).

But where and under what conditions would this new life be lived? Recall the teaching of Jesus. Its chief subject was the Kingdom of Heaven, which was to be established suddenly on the revelation of the Messiah from heaven. This double event would inaugurate a new age, the Messianic Age, for the Messiah would be the ruler of the new kingdom and into it all believers would be gathered. They would begin a new kind of life, for "flesh and blood cannot inherit the Kingdom of God," and it would be an altogether spiritual life, into which Jesus, the Messiah (so St Paul tells us a few years later), had already entered. He was the first-fruits; afterwards there would enter it they that were his. For there was a mystical link with him through their baptism, and in virtue of that union they were already, in a sense, in the new life with him. For redemption was more than liberation from sin; beyond that it was full membership of the new kingdom, and life in the new age and the kingdom was assured for them when they threw off the flesh by virtue of the indwelling of the Spirit. The Spirit is variously called the Spirit of God (Rom. viii. 14), the Spirit of the Messiah (*ibid.*, 9), or the Spirit of life in Jesus the Messiah (*ibid.*, v. 2).

It was a time of expectancy at present, but sooner or later, no one knew when, the Messiah would come with the voice of the archangel and with the trump of God, and all believers, whether risen from the grave or still living the earthly life, would stand before him, soon to be all caught up into the air and to be ever with the Lord. In his first letter to the Corinthians, St Paul adds that there must also be a contest with the powers of evil who, according to Jewish belief, were in control of the world. But having subdued these, even the last and worst of them, death which conquers every man, the Messiah will loyally submit himself, as before, to the Father who sent him to earth as his Vice-gerent, that God may be all in all (1 Thess. iv. 13–17; 1 Cor. xv. 23–28).

The doctrine of redemption was certainly St Paul's most important contribution to theology, if reinterpreted in the new light thrown on the current beliefs of the time about the Last Things, which has been obtained from the study of the Apocalyptic books. Modern opinion, indeed, since Luther and the Reformation has put another doctrine into the place of honour, viz. that of Justification by Faith. This was really a secondary polemical doctrine that was forced on St Paul, so to say, in defence of the sufficiency for redemption of the death of the Messiah. He saw himself confronted by the Jewish religion which had refused to accept Jesus the Messiah as Redeemer, and yet claimed to lead men to the same goal of redemption through obedience to the commandments of the Law. But St Paul's eschatology was universalistic. It offered salvation not merely to the Chosen People, but to every human being who accepted the Messiah as Redeemer, and he could not exclude Gentiles from that privilege because they refused to go to it through the gate of the Law. In that case they would claim to be forgiven by God because they had attained to righteousness by keeping the Law, at least to the best of their ability. But St Paul has to reject this arrangement because, first of all, no one can keep the whole Law (Rom. iii. 20-24); and secondly, because it was not God's intention that the Law should lead to salvation (Gal. iii. 16-29). God justifies freely, not on juristic grounds but by grace, as a giver, not as a judge. "By grace are ye saved, through faith, and that not of yourselves; it is the gift of God" (Eph. ii. 8). The teaching of Jesus was similarly universalistic; see Luke xiii. 23-30; and xiv. 15-24.

## 92 FROM CHRISTIANITY TO SPIRITUALISM

These passages raise another point in discussing St Paul's theology, viz. his acceptance of predestination. It was, however, not peculiar to him. It was a root doctrine of Judaism, expressed in the belief—which should make Christians wonder more than they do—that God had chosen the Jewish people and made them his favourite nation! This belief survives, but in an altered form, to-day. It is the foundation of the British-Israel propaganda. But why should intelligent Christians believe that the "lost" ten tribes of Israel, who disappeared from history after the exile, have been found again in the English—or should I say the British—people, the divine blessing which rested once on the lost tribes being replaced for their modern descendants by the glories of the British Empire?

We must surely look for the origin of this impossible belief about the All-Father and a small fraction of his children in the old Semitic Henotheism, which claimed Yahweh as the only god whom Israel could rightly worship, and that, too, in his own territory only. Israel acknowledged, at the same time, the real existence of the gods of their neighbours, and their ownership of their own territories.[1] Through the teaching of the prophets their Henotheism had by the end of the exile ripened into a noble Monotheism, but they still believed themselves to be Yahweh's favourites, and on that belief rested the

[1] See Judges xi. 12-33, Jephthah's message to the king of Ammon; 1 Sam. xxvi. 17-20, David's complaint to Saul about his persecution.

national hopes of Yahweh's intervention in history to save them from their national oppressors. It was this hope which enabled the Apocalyptic writers to build up the new Eschatology which we find accepted both by Jesus and St Paul. It is not necessary, then, to explain away the reason given in Mark iv. 10–12 for the use of parables, or the limiting clause "to them that are called according to his purpose" in St Paul's assurance that all things work together for good to those who love God (Rom. viii. 28). Believers, as a body, were predestined to membership of the kingdom; but Jesus in the discourse in Luke xiii. warned the favoured ones that virtuous people from the four quarters of the world might be preferred to them. Similarly St Paul, holding that redemption is a divine act of cosmic significance which provides for the human race a ready-made salvation—if I may so call it—which each individual has only to make his own by faith and obedience, cannot allow that Gentiles who are willing and able to win that salvation by offering the necessary faith and obedience should have imposed on them the extra and, in his opinion, quite unnecessary burden of obedience to a Law, even though the Law was alleged to be divine.

For the purposes of this book the foregoing short exposition of part of the teaching of St Paul may suffice. Readers who wish to study it further should do so in Dr Schweitzer's *The Mysticism of Paul the Apostle.*

CHAPTER V

# FROM JESUS TO CHRIST

In Chapters III and IV there are given pictures, however incomplete and poor, of Jesus the Prophet and Paul the Theologian. The former believes himself to be the Messiah, and that he will be manifested as such within the lifetime of some of those who listen to his teaching. He even declared to the High Priest that he would soon be seen by all men coming on the clouds of heaven. The latter is arrested in his active persecution of the heretics who believed in Jesus the Prophet, and by a sudden conversion is convinced that Jesus is alive in the other world, and not only so but is, what he claimed in life to be, the national Messiah. Developing this belief under the influence of his active brain and his deep religious feeling, he ends by creating a being who is ultimately known to every one as the Christian "Christ." What connection this Pauline figure has with the Prophet Jesus is not immediately clear, but nowadays the names Jesus and Christ are used indiscriminately as if there were no difference between them, and this not only by pious people who know no theology, but by preachers who usually know some, and even by theologians who claim to know a good deal.

This fact was commented on in an article entitled

"Jesus or Christ? An appeal for consistency," written for the *Hibbert Journal* of January 1909 by the Rev. R. Roberts of Bradford. The flood of comments which flowed in upon the Editor showed that this was a question on which thoughtful men were seeking light, and seventeen articles, not merely replying to Mr Roberts but "discussing the whole problem of the relation of the Jesus of history to the Christ of religion" appeared as a *Hibbert Journal Supplement* later in the year under the same title: "Jesus or Christ?"

To illustrate what is claimed for the Christ of to-day Mr Roberts quoted first Bishop Westcott of Durham:

"The Gospel of Christ Incarnate, the Gospel of the Holy Trinity in terms of human life, which we have to announce covers every imaginable fact of life to the end of time, and is new now as it has been new in all the past, new in its power, and new in its meaning, while the world lasts" (*Christus Consummator*, p. 171);

Then Principal Fairbairn, who speaks of the "Historical Christ" as "the Person that literature felt to be its loftiest ideal, Philosophy conceived as its highest personality, Criticism as its supreme problem, Theology as its fundamental datum, Religion as its cardinal necessity" (*Christ in Modern Theology*, p. 294);

And even the Unitarian Dr Drummond, in his Hibbert Lecture, "The Word made Flesh discloses to us, not some particular truth or requirement, but the very spirit and character of God, so far as we are able to apprehend it: for the Divine Thought is God Himself passing into manifestation, just as our speech is our own personality entering into communication with others" (*Via, Veritas, Vita*, p. 312).

From the article by the Rev. (now Canon) R. J. Campbell I quote the following: "Reduced to its simplest terms, therefore, we may say that the only part of the original Christ idea which has power with the modern mind is the thought of an ideal Man, the soul of the universal order, germinally present in every individual, and becoming increasingly manifest as time goes on in the perfecting of human relations. The Christ is a cosmic name so far as it stands for that in God which is becoming manifest in creation. It is a religious name in that it provides as an ideal for worship a humanity that is divine, and is the source and goal of our own. It is an ethical name. . . . It is a political and social name" (p. 187).

A quotation from Bishop Barnes' book *Should such a Faith Offend?* may perhaps be taken as fairly summing up the unhistorical views of East and West alike. "To the English Modernist the Incarnation is the fundamental fact of human history. . . . Christ appeared not only as the product of history but as its Lord. . . . He is the eternal Son and Wisdom of God, the Creator of all that is, who at a certain climax of history came down from heaven and was incarnate and made man. . . . Such a claim is of the essence of Christianity."

It is evident that there is a connection between the ideas in these quotations and the Fourth Gospel. That Gospel was written about the end of the first century, and gave the picture of a divine man so different from that of the Synoptists as to make Père Loisy say: "Il y a comme deux Christs." (It seems as if there were two Christs.) It was meant to help the reconciliation of Christianity with Greek philosophy, in which the title "Logos" (which means Word) was used as early as about 300 B.C. for the Wisdom of God, and is said to have been the Agent through whom He made the world.[1]

Why has this cosmic significance been given to the title "Christ?" The title is not Oriental in any way. It is Jewish, though Greek in form, being the Greek translation of the Hebrew Mashiach, or Messiah, that is, the Anointed One.

In his article in the *Hibbert Journal Supplement* Dr J. E. Carpenter, the well-known Unitarian theologian, gives a survey of the literature and ideas which influenced Jewish thought during the last century B.C., and which, he adds, provide the elements of a Christology. The *Supplement* was published in 1909, the year preceding the appearance in English of Dr Albert Schweitzer's great work *The Quest of the Historical Jesus*. Dr Carpenter alludes to Dr Schweitzer's

[1] See Sir Flinders Petrie's *Personal Religion in Egypt before Christianity* (Harper's Library of Living Thought, 1909).

assertion—made some years earlier in a preliminary study recently republished in England under the title of *The Mystery of the Kingdom of God*—that Jesus expected the revelation of the Messianic Kingdom before the Twelve could finish their missionary tour (Matt. x. 1–29), and says "that Jesus identified himself with the mysterious person who was to descend from the sky" (p. 148). He thus comes very near to the solution of the difficulty. He does not reach it, however, for want of the key idea, viz. the expectation of a new age ($αἰών$, æon) which was to be inaugurated with the revelation of the Messianic Kingdom. Into that new age with its supernatural life Jesus the Messiah (so St Paul taught a little later) had entered through his death and resurrection. Believers in him who were destined—and predestined—to membership of the kingdom but were still in the flesh could begin their membership by mystical union with him. Such mystical union was the very kernel of St Paul's own life and personal religion, which was a Christ-Mysticism, and complete study of the Synoptic Gospels and the Pauline epistles, taking into account the non-fulfilment of the promise of Jesus to appear again "sitting at the right hand of power, and coming on the clouds of heaven" (Matt. xxvi. 64), shows that "the Christ" came into existence as a purely imaginary figure created by the needs of St Paul's eschatology or doctrine of the Last Things.

Out of St Paul's Christ-Mysticism has developed

the orthodox Christ of the Apostles' and Nicene creeds. And is not the chief strength of the appeal which the Christian faith makes to-day to those "who profess and call themselves Christians" to be found in the belief, based on the experience of themselves and others, that they get help and guidance from "Christ" which are available to them from no other source? And is not that Christ, however skilfully adapted by Modernists to modern thought, extremely like the imaginary Pauline figure described above and in Chapter IV? It seems hardly too bold to say that the religion of the twentieth-century Christian may be, and often is, a Christ-Mysticism, just as St Paul's was.

This appeal to experience is felt to-day to be a very strong argument for the truth of Christianity, but does it not after all prove too much? For the development in Christian doctrine which has put such a wide gap between the Jewish Messiah and the Christian Christ is not the only important one which has come about since the fourth century. In the Roman Church the Virgin Mary has gradually been raised to a position which makes her very nearly equal in honour and power to her divine Son, and millions of Catholic Christians are quite convinced that they receive from her the comfort, guidance, and spiritual help which Protestants are equally certain that they receive, and can only receive, from Christ himself. This belief has been strengthened in our day by cures of diseases effected at Lourdes and other places, which are attributed to her agency.

But if the faith—or as Protestants mostly think it to be the credulity—of Catholics enables them to get from the B.V.M. the help which Protestants are equally sure that they get from Christ himself, would not that go no little way towards proving that she too is divine?

Is it really evidence of that? Is the B.V.M. really divine?

Or will she become so, if . . .?

And if the faith of Protestants finds, as it undoubtedly does find, more in the history of the Church and of theological doctrine to support it than does the corresponding faith in the B.V.M., is that a sufficient guarantee that even their faith is justifiable, and not really based on misinterpreted history?

For now we find a third claimant for the honour of being an exactly similar source of grace and power. Dr Schweitzer, having rescued the Historic Jesus from the pens of all the critics friendly or unfriendly, ends the Epilogue of his great book, *The Quest of the Historical Jesus*, with the tender and confident words: "He comes to us as One unknown, without a name, as of old by the lakeside He came to those men who knew not who He was. He speaks to us the same word. 'Follow thou me!' and sets us to the tasks which He has to fulfil in our time. He commands. And to those who obey Him, whether they be wise or simple, He will reveal Himself in the peace, the toils, the conflicts, the sufferings which they are privileged to experience in His fellowship, and, as an ineffable mystery, they shall learn by their own experience who He is."

And this unorthodox and unwelcome vindicator of the Historical Jesus finds support from a member of the least dogmatic body of present-day Christians. In this year's Swarthmore Lecture of the Society of Friends we read: "Who is this Christ? Who is this God of the Christians? Is he part of the real world in which we live, in the sense that, if we try to understand that world, he is something that we must take into account or else our understanding will be faulty and inadequate for the purposes of life? Or is he the fading image of a worn-out superstition? . . . The answer of Christian theology to these questions is to take us back nearly two thousand years to a country very different from our own and to a life in many ways simpler than ours, and to point to one Jesus. It asserts that Christ lives in the world to-day and that He and Jesus of Nazareth are one and the same. This is a most remarkable assertion, and no thinking man or woman can accept it as true without at once beginning to try to explain how such a thing could be. The explanations have been many and various, changing with changing methods of thought. . . .

"It is perhaps in the quietness of our meetings that we are most strongly drawn back to the one who pointed us to this way—to the simple-minded, strong-hearted Jesus, who taught us this secret of life. As we find his wisdom proved time and again in our experience, as over and over again we find that his words bring light to the dark places of our lives, our hearts are filled with gratitude to him as our leader and master. . . . Humbly and reverently, but with a great and joyous hope, we shall call him our friend." [1]

Perhaps this simplifies the problem, for we now have Catholics, Protestants, and wholly undogmatic Christians—a classification which may surely be said to include the whole body of those who "profess and call themselves Christians"—all finding their chief reward for being Christians in the grace and help they get from either Jesus, or "Christ," or the B.V.M. Is it possible that they can all three be right? It seems unlikely, even supposing what is also unlikely, that we can agree upon a reliable criterion, acceptable to all three parties, by which to decide their rightness or wrongness.

But there is happily a logical means of escaping from the need of making any such decision. The help received by the holders of these varied forms of belief may come to them all from some source which is different from that which they severally imagine it to be. It may come direct from God, the All-Father himself, and such a belief would be quite in accordance with the teaching of the Sermon

[1] *Christ, Yesterday and To-day*, the Swarthmore Lecture, by Geo. B. Jeffery, F.R.S. (Allen & Unwin, 1934, pp. 10 and 46).

on the Mount (see Matt. v. 43-48; vi. 25 to end; vii. 7-12; and *cp.* Acts xiv. 15-17 and xvii. 24-28). Only in that case we must surely believe that the help is available for all God's children, whether they be Christians or Jews, Mahommedans or Buddhists or Hindus, agnostics or even atheists. And if so, it is obviously not a reward for Christian piety, nor indeed for the holding of any particular form of religious belief.

That such divine help can come through the Jesus of tradition and the creeds we can easily believe, and even if we do not claim to understand how, we may consider the faith that so many Christians repose in him to be fully justified. About the B.V.M. nothing need be said here. But the title Christ to anyone who reflects on life and religion is mysterious, and we cannot acquiesce in it as an unexplainable mystery.

Let us consider it in the light of what has been said in Chapters III and IV, and examine more carefully what St Paul's share in creating it was. It has been already shown that the first thing to which St Paul was converted was to a conviction that Jesus was at any rate alive in the world above, from which the Messiah was universally expected to appear. But the fact that he was alive did not prove true what he had claimed before the High Priest, viz. that he was "the Messiah, the Son of the Blessed," nor what he had promised in the same answer, viz. that he would prove it by appearing at the right hand of power on the clouds of heaven.

Dr Schweitzer, who is a historian as well as a theologian, has shown, on good grounds, that Jesus did believe himself to be "the Messiah-to-be." That was his Messianic secret, and St Paul knew so much. It was the claim to be—in any form or at any time—the Messiah that provoked the zealous Pharisee to persecution. But did not the failure of Jesus to keep his promise and to manifest himself in that way prove that his belief was mistaken? Suppose that it was a mistake, and then look at subsequent events in the light of it. We can understand them quite well through our knowledge of Spiritualism to-day. For Spiritualists generally are agreed that Jesus had a considerable amount of psychic power, and that some at least of the Apostles were similarly endowed. For at the Transfiguration he was changed in appearance himself, and Moses and Elijah could show themselves in materialised form by power drawn from him and probably from the three Apostles too. Similarly he appeared in a wholly materialised form to Cleopas and his companion on the journey to Emmaus, where he disappeared suddenly at the end of the meal by dematerialising. During the time occupied by these doings he had shown himself to Peter, but probably clairvoyantly, which was no doubt the case when he showed himself to Mary in the garden and forbade her to touch him.

These appearances were by no means equivalent to such a manifestation as believers were certainly expecting, but they were so unusual and surprising that they sufficed to avert a critical examination of the reasons why the promised revealing from heaven did not take place. The same may be said of St Paul. His anxiety to get to Damascus for the patriotic persecution of the heretics was so strong that his sudden arrest outside the town, the temporary blindness, and the voice from heaven convinced him that Jesus was alive, but also prevented him from remembering in his excitement that the claim of Jesus to be the Messiah had not yet been proved by the fulfilment of his promise to appear on the clouds of heaven. And in his excitement he jumped at two conclusions, both of which were over-hasty. The first was that the Messiah had really come at last, however strange the way was in which he had shown himself, and although it was not what Jesus had promised. The second was that the new enthusiasm and spiritual power which he felt within him were imparted to him by this new person, who became from that hour the centre of his personal religion, and also the crowning element in the Messianic eschatology which during the remaining thirty years of his life he developed into what became, through the work of several generations of theologians and teachers, the Nicene theology.

St Peter and the main body of believers travelled more slowly in the same direction, starting from "Jesus of Nazareth, a MAN approved of God"

(Acts ii. 20),[1] and therefore raised from the dead —by a special exertion of divine power, be it noted! —to be Lord and Messiah (*ibid.*, 24 and 36). He is not pre-existent in heaven, however, for "the heavens must receive him until the time of the restoration of all things"; that is, till the revelation of the Messianic Kingdom and the destruction of the material world. From Acts xiv. 23 onwards the title of Lord ($κύριος$) is freely given to him, although throughout this book of the Acts, and the Greek translation of the Old Testament, that word is used as the title of God himself. And the process ends (under the leadership of the active mind of St Paul) by the clothing of the Carpenter of Nazareth with all the attributes belonging to the Jewish Messiah, viz. pre-existence, a share in creation, Judgeship, Sonship, so that he becomes practically a second God.

Now that we have obtained this explanation about the least known and understood of the three personalities who are accepted by Christians as undoubtedly channels of divine grace, shall we find that Spiritualism can help us to come to some decision as to how they can all three be rightly accepted as such, even though Protestants do scout the claims which Roman Catholics make for the B.V.M. and to a lesser extent for their canonised saints?

I believe it can, but it will be better to leave its answer to our difficulty till some of the elementary

[1] *Cp.* Acts xvii. 30 f.

facts of Spiritualism have been put before readers, some of whom may not yet have come to any final conclusion or conviction about its truth and value, while others may not even have begun to think seriously about its nature and its claims on our acceptance.

CHAPTER VI

## SPIRITUALISM

In Chapter I a very short account was given of the origin of modern Spiritualism in the middle of the last century, and the testimony was quoted of one great man of Science (better known in another connection) who was converted by facts, the truth and reality of which he could not doubt (Chap. I, p. 15). Prof. Richet in his *Thirty Years of Psychic Research* says: "The idolatry of current ideas was so dominant at that time that no pains were taken either to verify or to refute Sir Wm. Crookes's statements. Men were content to ridicule them, and I avow with shame that I was among the wilfully blind. Instead of admiring the heroism of a recognised man of science who dared then, in 1872, to say that there really are phantoms that can be photographed, and whose heart-beats can be heard, I laughed."

In token of his repentance he dedicated his book to Sir Wm. Crookes and F. W. H. Myers.

Scores of other men's testimony could be quoted, but I will only mention Sir Oliver Lodge without quoting him, and then assume as proved the two main facts of Spiritualism. The first is that our spirits survive what we call death, and continue their life in a spirit world with an organised social life of its own in many ways like that of ours on earth. The second is that communication is possible in both directions between these two worlds.

The branch of science called Physics has made enormous progress in recent years, and it now offers for our acceptance facts which are almost unimaginable about the physical universe. It tells us that what we call matter is not really solid, but is made up of atoms which are composed of electrons revolving at immense speed round a centre which is called a proton, and that these atoms exist, and move in perfectly orderly fashion in an ocean of space which is not empty, but filled with a marvellous substance called ether. The waves of ether undulate through space at various speeds, and thus are produced currents of power which manifest themselves in various ways, producing light, heat, sound, magnetism, etc. For example, light-waves travel, as we have long known, at a rate of 186,000 miles a second, and recently there have been discovered other waves which travel far faster and can be transformed into words and can be transmitted through our atmosphere. Thus the ether is the medium between material things and our senses, and matter may be said shortly to be composed of ether and electricity. The ether of space is the link between the world of matter and the world of spirit, for it is the substance common to both, and we can explain to ourselves the nature and action of the spirit world by the analogy of the physical.

The ether has for its different uses different rates of vibration, and those of the spirit world are infinitely faster than those of our world, so that to most people that world is unperceivable, and they can neither see nor hear its inhabitants. Yet to those inhabitants their world is as real and solid as ours is to us, and they can see our world and us with varying degrees of clearness, just as we can perceive their world with varying degrees of clearness *if we have any psychic power*. Those of us who have this power in abundant measure we call "mediums," and ordinary people are, speaking generally, deaf and blind to spirit communications without the presence of a medium, just as we all are to the etheric waves which give us wireless communications, unless we have a suitable "medium" in the form of an apparatus which has a "transmitter" and a "receiver," commonly called a "loud speaker."[1]

This analogy of the physical world makes us bold to suppose that there is a spiritual ether through which currents of spiritual power come to us, and that these manifest themselves to our spirit and soul, *i.e.* to our real personality, according to our capacity for using and benefiting by them. They come to us direct, or at least they can do so, but we, *i.e.* the majority of us, connect them with our religion.

[1] For an admirable exposition of the methods of communication between the two worlds see Findlay's *On the Edge of the Etheric*, 1931. The nature of our physical world and the analogy with the spirit world is well described in the first three chapters of the book.

That, of course, varies with the country of which we are natives and the religion prevailing in it, with our early surroundings and education also, and with our later experience. The great personalities; too, of each religion, from whom, or at least through whom, the power or help from above seems to reach us, vary accordingly.

Returning to the question at issue in the last chapter (pp. 102) we can now give the solution and can say that the three varieties of Christians are all of them right: Protestants in looking to Christ, Catholics in looking to the Virgin Mary, and others in looking to the Historic Jesus. But having gone so far we must go further and allow that all God's children are, or may be, just as right as Christians; that Mahommedans are helped through the Koran, Buddhists through Gautama the Buddha, and Hindus through Krishna.

But what brought all these religions into existence? More than one cause, no doubt; but one cause was surely the belief that they offered at least a provisional answer to the questions: "What is there behind the heavy curtain of death?" and "What happens to us in the Black Beyond?"

Does this apply to Christianity as well as to the other religions, or is the former an exception because it is a religion of redemption with the efficacy of that redemption guaranteed as being the voluntary work of a unique Person, a God-man, who "for us men and for our salvation came down from heaven," doing so because "God so loved the world that he gave his only begotten Son that whosoever believeth in him should not perish but should have everlasting life"? That has been the universal belief of Christendom, but the antiquity of the belief does not guarantee its truth. The above quotation is from the Nicene Creed, which was drawn up in the fourth century at a time when America and Australia were undiscovered, and the civilised world of the West knew very little about Russia, Siberia, and the Far East. Science had indeed been born in the Greek world, thanks to the inquiring mind of Thales of Miletus (c. 625 B.C.), but the Christian world contented itself some seven centuries later with what the Old Testament told it of Man's origin, and of the origin of the sin for which redemption was supposed to be necessary. The doctrine of the Atonement was evidently based directly on the story of Creation and the Fall in Genesis ii. and iii., and was a not unreasonable solution of the dilemma latent in the Hebrew story, *so long as that story was believed to be true.* But we know now that Man has existed for some 300,000 years on this little globe, and his existence in the future we are told to measure in millions of years.

Moreover the doctrine, as stated in terms of the Genesis story and the Synoptic Gospels, became more complicated through the conversion of St Paul, and the conviction to which he came over-hastily that the voice which spoke to him, and was no doubt the voice of Jesus, was at the same time the voice of the Being whom Jesus had in life claimed to be, viz. the Jewish Messiah. Thus a second Being, divine or semi-divine, found its way into Christian theology, a Being whom St Paul held to be God's agent in the work of human redemption, and who therefore had to be identified or reconciled in some way or other with Jesus of Nazareth, who a few years before had died upon the Cross for the same purpose.[1] This Being, the Messiah, was a necessary

[1] Or is this last statement a putting upon the death of Jesus an interpretation which is indeed the traditional one, but which was not in fact given to it quite so early?

For firstly, in the Synoptic record—as corrected by criticism and with allowance for the Gospels having appeared in their present, final form perhaps a generation later—the only passages which contain, or seem to contain, that belief, viz. the description by Jesus himself, of his death as "a ransom for many" (Mark x. 45), and the words of institution at the Last Supper, provide surely a very slight foundation for that belief, even if interpreted in the traditional way. Moreover, the reply of Jesus to the High Priest (Mark xiv. 61-2) is not exactly what we should have anticipated from one who was on the eve of dying, as Christians have always believed, to be a sacrifice for all mankind.

Further, in his speech on the day of Pentecost (Acts ii. 14 ff.), Peter begins his reference to Jesus by calling him "a MAN, approved by God unto you by . . ." and ends by claiming for him nothing more than that God "hath made him both Lord and Messiah." For proof of his statement he appeals to the Book of Joel and Psalms xvi. and cx. There is no hint of any belief in Jesus as a universal Saviour.

Moreover, St Paul at the moment of his conversion certainly had no such belief about Jesus. Indeed he was persecuting his followers just because Jesus himself had falsely (so St Paul thought) claimed to be the Messiah. In the next few days, however, at Damascus St Paul came to the conviction that Jesus was the Messiah after all (Acts ix. 22). By this he must

character in St Paul's cosmic doctrine of redemption, and traditional theology identifies him without any critical questioning with Jesus, by adding to the human name, Jesus, the eschatological title of Messiah (in Hebrew) or (in the better-known Greek language) χριστός or Christ. In this it follows St Paul, indeed, who in his earliest letter, the First to the Thessalonians, written in A.D. 49, praises the converts at Thessalonica for their "patience of hope in the Lord Jesus Christ," that is "the Lord Jesus, the Messiah, before our God and Father" (1 Thess. i. 3).

But the study of the Apocalyptic Books has made known the want of historical foundation for the late-Jewish eschatology, and our fuller knowledge, given us by science, of the past history and experience

have meant the man in whom the Messiah, pre-existing in heaven according to his own and the general Jewish belief, had become incarnate so as to enter the dominion of sin (chap. iv. p. 86). This interpretation of the death would be an obvious one to him, for it filled a gap in his theory of redemption, which required a human personality in whom the Redeemer, the Messiah, could become incarnate for the completion in this world of his redeeming work. Further, since St Paul was the strongest personality and the best educated among the Apostles, as well as the most original and progressive teacher among them, it is not unreasonable to attribute to him the further effects of the Crucifixion which belong to the traditional belief, so that it provided a way of salvation by vicarious sacrifice which believers could easily understand and would be only too ready to rely on. Thus the human side also of his doctrine of redemption was completed, and nothing but faith in a divine-human Saviour was now needed in those who desired to benefit by the salvation accomplished for them by him.

of the human race makes it at least doubtful whether we can take seriously the belief that such a world-wide atonement was necessary or even possible. Such a belief seems to belong to the childhood of the race, and from that childhood we are now emerging.

Spiritualism, too, has developed so much since its rebirth in 1848 that we have many messages given from the Beyond through Stainton Moses and other reliable mediums, which encourage us and help us to criticise and amend the prevalent Christian beliefs. This root doctrine of the Atonement is condemned in these messages as misleading, and dangerous also to Man's efforts to grow in character and spirituality. It cuts at the root of the Fifth Principle of Spiritualism—Personal Responsibility.

"The ideal of Jesus, the Christ, is no more like the human notion with its accessories of atonement and redemption as men have grasped them, than was the calf ignorantly carved by the ancient Hebrews (Exodus xxxii. 1-6), like the God who strove to reveal himself to them. Salvation is not a reconciliation of sin-stained humanity to a holy and angry God, purchased by the sacrifice of His sinless Son, but a higher at-one-ment in the ennobling of the nature, the purifying of the spirit, the making of the human and the divine ONE in aim and purpose—the drawing up of man's spirit, even while in the flesh, nearer and nearer to the Divine" (Stainton Moses, *Spirit Teachings*, pp. 69, 70).

If, then, the central doctrine of Christianity is misleading and dangerous, it can hardly have a God-man for its source. The doctrine of the Incarnation must go, and with it that of the Virgin Birth. The Resurrection has already been explained, and the Ascension can be explained similarly for any who are troubled about it. It would have been a fitting end for the earthly career of a "Christ," but is quite unnecessary for that of Jesus, the Prophet of Nazareth. The future Judgment of the Last Day is also evidently an adaptation of the Messianic Judgment which was to be held of quick and dead alike when the Messianic Kingdom was revealed (Matt. xxv. 31–46).

What is written in the three preceding chapters shows, when considered as a whole, that Protestants who complain of being asked to accept "Churchianity" when they look for Christianity have much reason on their side, even if they cannot explain why or how. It should be clear now that what is thus denounced as "Churchianity" is really "Paulinism," that is, the Pauline element in Christianity. This grew up on the basis of St Paul's identification of the Jesus, whose followers he was persecuting, with the Jewish Messiah, who was an imaginary being with no basis at all in history.

That in Pauline Christianity there should be a priesthood was natural; Judaism had one, and almost every other religion. The sacraments have been explained indirectly already: Baptism was the gate of entry into the mystic union with Christ, and the Eucharist was an anticipation of the life of the New Age (Mark xiv. 25; 1 Cor. xi. 26; see iii. 12*a*, note). The second Person of the Trinity having disappeared, it is useless to personify the Spirit of God so as to be a third Person in a Trinity, but the reality behind it we can see in the spiritual power spoken of in Chapter V.

Now let us give the answer of Spiritualism to Man's old, old question: "What is there behind the curtain of death? And what happens to us in the Black Beyond?"

Let me preface our answer with part of Mrs Barbauld's beautiful little poem, *Life*, which throws a tender and encouraging glow round what is still regarded by most people as "the last enemy to be destroyed."

### LIFE

Life, I know not what thou art,
But know that thou and I must part;
And when, or how, or where we met
I own to me's a secret yet.

  Life! we've been long together
Through pleasant and through cloudy weather!
'Tis hard to part when friends are dear—
Perhaps 'twill cost a sigh, a tear;
Then steal away, give little warning,
  Choose thine own time;
Say not Good Night, but in some brighter clime
  Bid me Good Morning.

For Spiritualism tells us that death is nothing more formidable than entrance into a spirit world which is as real and far more beautiful than ours, and there follows it automatically and immediately for each individual a judgment. But there is no judge, nor any formal trial. Our past life is our judge, for there passes before our inward eye a complete record of that past life, vivid and accurate as the pictures in a cinematograph. And that record decides the place for which the course of his life here has fitted each one. He finds himself, too, in the society of others in the same stage of development as himself, unless the state of his soul requires that he be for a time in darkness and solitude or, worse still, in the company of sinners more abandoned than himself; discarnate human spirits mostly, but, it may be, elementals also who have never been human.

> For there is what may be called a hell,
>   Since God is just;
> But it is for a time only, till penitence comes,
>   Since God is love.

In that world the divine justice and the divine love are inseparable, like the concave and the convex of a curve, and the judgment is passed on deeds, not on beliefs. No one is asked what he has believed, but all are asked how far they have practised the Golden Rule. The religion of the future may perhaps be called Christianity, but it will be

Christianity reduced to its simplest terms. It will be just the Religion of Love, as taught by Jesus.

In conclusion let me finish with a few of the messages received from the Beyond. But it may help some readers to say clearly that Spiritualism includes three things:

A. Phenomena.
B. Belief in survival.
C. Intelligent communication with the Spirit world.

To the majority of people at present that intercourse means getting comforting information from or about relatives or friends who have passed over. But it should be understood that such "departed" ones are often, though by no means always, anxious to communicate with those whom they have had to leave. Numberless cases are on record when they have had the joy of giving warning or useful information to those still in the earth-life. For example, a boy was recently found lying dead, evidently shot by the gun he was carrying. Suicide was suspected, but he was able through a medium to convince his parents and others that his death was purely an accident.

But for those who on earth were thinkers, teachers, writers, or in public life, one way in which they can continue their work is by inspiring ideas in those who are still on earth, or sending messages which may help to raise those of mankind whom they can reach out of the false ideas inherited from the past, and from the gross and terrible materialism and selfishness which are the cause of nearly all the poverty and misery in the world to-day, not to mention the insane and criminal folly of armaments and wars. And these would-be "helpers and friends of mankind" are organised for their work.

"I have become a member of a Fellowship," writes Prof. Wm. James, once Professor of Philosophy and Psychology at Harvard,[1] "composed of individuals who recognise the vital importance of rousing your world to the consciousness of spiritual being. We know the YOU of which you remain in ignorance, and which, in some cases, you do not wish to know. We also realise that, unless you recognise and become your real selves, your world will have some very difficult trials to pass through. You may ask: 'What authority have you for interfering with life on earth?' My Friends, I have, nothing whatever to do with the changes which are about to take place. I am guided by greater souls who are gifted with spiritual wisdom. We seek their advice, knowing that it is God's wish that we should help you. We shall make every possible use of the people through whom we can reach your world, and we have all hopes of realising our opportunities. There is great need for co-operation on your side, vital need, and the future of humanity depends on you."

[1] In Miss M. V. Underhill's *Your Infinite Possibilities*, pp. 27 f.

This message and the extracts given further on suggest the answer to the question how we are to judge messages when they come from spirits about whom no personal or otherwise evidential details are available to assure us that the messages are genuine. We must test them by the light of reason, considering whether they are consistent with what we know from other reliable sources, and are in accordance with our moral ideals, so that we can give them at least such provisional credence as we give to what is told us about the past by historians, about nature by men of science, and by travellers about parts of the world that we have not visited ourselves.

For it is unreasonable to expect that passing into the spirit world will effect some quasi-miraculous change in our mentality. The ignorant or simple-minded will not be made into wonders of learning by "passing over" any more than a bishop is made into a theologian of the first rank by his university making him an Hon. D.D. Illusions held here persist there till they are corrected, as they do with us, so that there is a variety of views in that world very similar to what there is here. No doubt learned and intelligent persons who pass over may soon be able to send over messages with new ideas, and those who hold progressive views here will no doubt be more ready than others to accept such communications as genuine and welcome.

If, as many now believe to be possible, we are to

get reliable help from this source, it can only be by patient collection of evidence and unprejudiced valuation of it, and that needs time. So let us not be in a hurry, but be time-thinkers as well as space-thinkers, and, since psychic science is still in its infancy, let us keep our minds as open as we can for what it may be able to teach us in our small fraction of the immeasurable period of existence which lies before our race. And we must think backwards as well as forwards. If man has existed for some 300,000 years on a globe which is perhaps 2000 million years old, and has taken all that time to rise to what he is now, even from something already much higher than his ultimate source in the "inert atoms of the primeval slime," then, as Prof. T. H. Huxley wrote in 1863 in *Man's Place in Nature*: "Thoughtful men, once escaped from the blinding influence of traditional prejudice, will find in the lowly stock from which man has sprung the best evidence of the splendour of his capacities, and will discern in his long progress through the past a reasonable ground of faith in his attainment of a noble future."

There follow some passages giving information which may reasonably be accepted as possibly correct, and which, though from different sources, are fairly consistent. It is to be hoped that the passages will at least set readers thinking, and then each must judge for himself. For their sources see p. 130.

A. "Religion, the spirit's healthful life, has two aspects—the one pointing to God, the other to man. . . . We do not recognise any need of propitiation towards this God. We reject as false any notion of the Divine Being vindictively punishing a transgressor or requiring a vicarious sacrifice for sin. . . . God as we know Him in the operation of His laws is perfect, pure, loving, the centre of life and love, the object of our admiration, never of our dread. None has seen Him, nor are we content with the metaphysical sophistries with which prying curiosity and subtle speculation have obscured the primary conception of God among men. The first conception even with you is grander, nobler, more sublime. We know nothing of the potency of blind faith or credulity. We know, indeed, the value of a trustful, receptive spirit, free from the littleness of perpetual suspicion. Such is godlike, and draws down angel guidance. But we denounce that most destructive belief that faith or assent to dogmatic statements have power to erase the traces of transgression; that an earthly lifetime of vice and sloth and sin can be wiped away, and the spirit stand purified by the blind acceptance of a creed. Such teaching has debased more souls than anything to which we can point. Nor do we teach that there is a special efficacy in any one belief to the exclusion of others. We know, as you do not, the circumstances which decide to what special form of faith a mortal shall give his adherence. . . .

"You will learn, too, that all revelation is given through a human channel, and consequently cannot but be tinctured in some measure with human error. No revelation is of plenary inspiration. None can demand credence on any but rational grounds. . . . Weigh what is said; if it is commended by reason, receive it; if not, reject it. If what is put before you be prematurely said, and you are unable to accept it, then in the name of God put it aside and cling to aught that satisfies your soul and helps its forward progress. The time will come when what we lay before you of divine truth will be valued among men."

B. "You ask me a question [about God] which none of us who have been here for centuries can reply to. We know far more than you do. We have lived in many different worlds, and have gained by the memory of all our past existences, which is collective memory, but God, as you speak of Him, is as mysterious here as He is there. . . ." And here "there are no religions as you conceive them. Religions on earth are the different coats of paint with which you cover God till you can no longer see Him. God appears to us here as a most wonderful jewel; the many coarse coats of paint with which you cover Him on earth affect your vision so that you cannot recognise Him in the end. Here there are no creeds and no sects. We worship God in appreciation and thanksgiving. We worship Him every moment of the day. I feel at one with

Him. Christ is the highest expression of God on this plane. Here there are no Jews and no Roman Catholics. Their differences on earth have withered. God and His works are patent here to everyone. On the earth it is all symbolism. One sees God in candles and robes, another in music, and another in words. The gorgeous display which seems God to one is anathema to another, but the trouble is that each demands that his conception shall be held by the other. God is infinite. These people are finite, and have tried to express God as finite. To me it is easy to see God in a flower. Every beautiful day seems as if God has opened His eyes. There are meeting places here to help those who have lately passed over to worship, but not to argue."

C. "I can tell you about Christ here, but you must put Christ as you know him far from your mind. I speak of him as we think of him here. He is a Son of God; so are all of you. But he has more of the spirit than you have. He is a great thinker, a prophet also, but his ideas are not the ideas you have made use of simply because his spirit could not penetrate the thick crust of the world's selfish lust of gain." "He is regarded as the greatest of the prophets over here; not as a deity to be worshipped but as an artist rather—a lover and a philosopher as well, for his philosophy, which is that of love and sacrifice, is as old as the world. And yet he clothed it in a manner which gave it a new beauty and ecstasy for those who were able to follow his meaning. But in the course of time, and even quite soon after he had made his last psychic impression on the world, men had entirely changed all this. It came from themselves, not from his teaching, for that is the source of the sudden and vivid flashes of light which lumine this world from time to time. These flashes cast gleams of brilliant light, but they leave behind them a deeper shadow. Here Christ is still a unity—a single influence. He shines as brightly here as he did in the world, and throws light on his own particular problems. Not on the universal problem, for only the great multitude of sages, artists, poets, and lovers can deal with this cosmos problem."

D. "My mind was quite a blank regarding life after death. I did not give it a thought; in fact, I was quite prepared for, and rather enjoyed the idea of a long, long sleep—in other words, total extinction.

"My passing out was rather sudden, and the extraordinary feeling of the expulsion of my real self from my outer body is an unforgettable experience. To my great surprise I then became aware of familiar faces and friends, and I thought momentarily I was in a dream state; but by degrees the reality of the situation forced itself upon me, and I was conscious that I was now living in a world utterly unknown to me—a world that no flights of imagination could ever have pictured for me.

"I am still amazed at its vastness, its beauty, its

homelike atmosphere, the various institutions, its unerring laws, its order and discipline, its broad thoroughfares, stately houses, and magnificent scenery.

"It is a human world where human people live, yet it is a heavenly world in which there is an entire lack of commercial competition, and all seem to live in harmony and peace; yet it is a world of progress and advancement, far ahead of the world I have left.

"As yet I have not seen much, but what I have seen fills me with wonder and amazement, and I bow in reverence to the Great Mind who has brought this scheme of life into existence.

"May I add that I am still following my old earth duties; the curriculum is the same, only upon spiritual lines, and I have been appointed senior master of an academy. At last I seem to have found my ideal life, and I wish I could make it clear to all what a beautiful thing indeed is that grim spectre miscalled death. To me it has been a gate of life, and not only has my body been rejuvenated, but my whole mental make-up seems to have an added brightness and lightness; in fact I feel full of energy, youth, ambition, and happiness."

E. "I am comparatively speaking a new-comer, but I am filled with awe and reverence for the Great Mind who has devised this great scheme of life, and I only wish I could make those whom I love on earth acquainted with this wonderful state of existence.

"I would also like to make clear to all on earth the reality of life after death. I cannot expect people to take my word entirely, but I have at heart only the interests of those whom I am trying to reach; I want all to know that they are watched by those who are living here, and who are trying to help them along the difficult path of life.

"It has also been taught me that we ourselves are personally responsible for all our omissions and commissions, and we cannot lay the burden of our misdeeds on a loving Christ nor can we expect forgiveness without personal atonement. For our sins we are held personally responsible, and we have to take the blame and work out our own salvation. No bolstering of creeds can help us, and as far as we consciously or unconsciously acted we are responsible. Of course many act from sheer ignorance, and all these degrees are taken into consideration, but the lot of the conscious evil-doer is far from pleasant here."

F. "On my arrival in the world of spirit I became greatly interested in the other people, many of whom had just left their physical bodies. We were the same inwardly as we had been on earth. I found that the sort of people who had been unprogressive in the world we had left behind were still sticky over here. Those who had realised some individuality and progress opened out to the new life and its privileges with greater ease.

"I had some satisfaction in finding that the preparatory work I had done gave me more initiative and power to progress than the average person. But I knew that I had immense gaps to bridge over, great truths to learn, principles and laws to understand. So I set to work to discover what I needed to know and be in this life. In the main I have followed the same lines of study which I had pursued in your world. I have sought for truth about man's being and becoming. . . . You have many difficulties and ills which are the direct result of disregarding the laws of progress. We are overwhelmed with good people who have to be instructed in the elements of personality and character, which they should have acquired during life on earth.

"My friends, it is time that you realised the value of human experience with a view to profiting by it during the Hereafter. All that we experience can be turned to good account if we know how to render it in spiritual values as well as in material ones. Many people have wasted life on earth simply because they saw nothing but the material values in life.

"Nonentities!—have you ever realised that those who have not grown into spiritual beings are nonentities? How many there are, alas! well we know; for the majority of people arrive here with no reason at all for being; they know not what they are.

"To me individuality means the human being who has developed character, will, personality, and many attributes and prerogatives of soul which enable him to express his real self; then he becomes an individual, not otherwise."

## SOURCES OF THE EXTRACTS

A. *Spirit Teachings*, by the Rev. Stainton Moses (M.A.Oxon.), pp. 69-70.
B. H. D. Bradley's *Towards the Stars*, bk. iii. chap. ii. p. 241, and bk. i. chap. xiii. p. 137.
C. *Ibid.*, bk. iii. chap. vi. pp. 262 ff.
D. and E. *Talks with Friends of Bench and Bar*, by a retired Public Servant through trance mediumship.
D. Foreword, by Dr Blake Odgers, K.C., p. 23.
E. Foreword, by Mr Justice Bray, p. 22.
F. *Your Infinite Possibilities*, by Margaret V. Underhill, pp. 24 ff. Almost the whole of this book was dictated from the Beyond by W. James, formerly Professor of Philosophy at Harvard University, through automatic writing, since February 1923.

The first extract is offered as an excellent statement of principles, and if it upsets the common readiness to accept current Christian doctrine as infallibly true, it at any rate leaves everyone free to live in this imperfect world by any honestly held belief, even if it be a very imperfect view in the light of truth as a whole.

Extract C confirms the view in Chapter III that Jesus of Nazareth was not one person of a Triune Deity, incarnate in a human personality, but the world's greatest moral teacher. It supports the view of Dr Schweitzer that he is that because he first preached in any completeness "the religion of love" without any dogma except what was part of the eschatological background underlying the Synoptic Gospels. That background was only temporary, but it explains why primitive Christianity waited for a century—but only for so long—with the expectation of a Second Coming of the Messiah, or "Christ." Jesus' religion of love is independent also of the Hellenistic world-view which succeeded the late-Jewish, and again of the mediæval worldview of a world governed by the two divinely commissioned vice-gerents of the Almighty, the Emperor and the Pope. Nor is it upset or made unnecessary by the scientific world-view of to-day, which tells us that our solar system is only one among many millions in the great universe, and that there are quite possibly many other races of rational beings on other planets, some more, some less, advanced than we are.

CHAPTER VII

# VALUES

"WHENEVER we dig below the incidental trappings of a society to the underlying structure, we find that this is the embodiment of a set of beliefs concerning man and his world, and our beliefs and the habits moulded on them often lag behind human sensitiveness. They tend to be survivals based on more primitive attitudes to the world. Social traditions do not, in fact, change as quickly as material circumstances. Hence it is likely to be obsolete social traditions rather than fundamental human characteristics that bar the way to those progressive adaptations to changing conditions which alone can secure to man a reasonable chance of happiness."

So wrote Prof. A. E. Heath in the Preface to his course of B.B.C. lectures called: *Thinking Aloud: the Place of Reflection in Civilisation*; and his plea for progress in thought as well as in material civilisation applies to religious thought as well as to secular, so long, at any rate, as the education and evolution of man's inner spiritual life has not reached its goal. It certainly has not reached it yet, and while it is a commonplace to say we are entering on a new age in material progress, is it not also true that the advance of thought is bringing us into a new age of progress in moral and religious matters?

# VALUES

It is only three-quarters of a century since Darwin published his *Descent of Man*, but what changes since then! His cotemporary, Dr Russel Wallace, published a generation ago a book called *The Wonderful Century*, in which he enumerated and described twenty-six notable discoveries or inventions of the nineteenth century, while he could name only eleven similar important and valuable ones made during all preceding history. And during the present century science has given us numberless further novelties, big and little, which have done more still to revolutionise our thought and action.

But Christianity was born in an unscientific and simple time, and it claimed to be based on a continuous revelation which had culminated in a Person who was at once human and divine. This claim had been developed and explained sufficiently for that uncritical age within two generations of the Crucifixion. There was opposition to it, indeed, but not from science. The opposition came from the holders of current religious and philosophic ideas, partly Hellenic, partly Eastern, working through various schools of thought and religious associations, which tried to blend their own ideas with Christianity. Most of them were condemned as heretical, and they did not prevent Christianity from becoming in the fourth century, when it emerged from its formative period, the accepted religion of the West and the Near East.

Probably by no other means than this claim to have a special divine origin could Christianity have won its way to victory over the Græco-Roman paganism, and, in the Dark Ages which followed, over the Nordic tribes which settled in Europe in the fifth and following centuries to lay the foundations of the different nations of to-day.

"The old Saxon and Danish faith was a religion of barbarism with no elements in itself of further progress; it was merely a traditional expression of racial character, not an outside force at work upon that character. At a meeting of the Northumbrian Witan when the question was discussed of whether the Christian missionaries under Paullinus should be welcomed or not, one of the thegns urged that they should be, saying to King Edwine: 'The present life of man upon earth, O King, seems to me, in comparison of that time which is unknown to us, like to the swift flight of a sparrow through the house where you sit at supper in winter, with your Eldermen and Thegns, while the fire blazes in the midst and the hall is warmed, but the wintry storms of rain and snow are raging abroad. The sparrow, flying in at one door and immediately out at another, whilst he is within is safe from the wintry tempest; but after a short space of fair weather he immediately vanishes out of your sight, passing from winter into winter again. So this life of man appears for a little while, but of what is to follow or what went before we know nothing at all. If, therefore, this new doctrine tells us something more certain, it seems justly to deserve to be followed.'

"The Christian missionaries had, indeed, an immense advantage in bringing a clear-cut cosmogony and definite doctrines about heaven and hell, how to attain the one and avoid the other." [1]

Christianity may indeed reasonably advance a claim to be the religion which is best fitted to become that of the whole world. But on what ground? Not that it has a specially divine origin, but that it is the most truly moral. It not only puts a high ideal of character before the world, and shows "how to attain to heaven and to avoid hell"; but it also has an activist ethic, and urges its adherents not only to *be* good but to *do* good; not only to accept the morality of the Gospel but to put it into practice, assuring them at the same time of supernatural power and help in doing so. And this promise has been continuously fulfilled from the days which followed Pentecost to the work done to-day by the Salvation Army and the Christian Student Movement.

"But though the power is the same (says Prof. Percy Gardner), I do not think that the old explanations will satisfy the modern spirit. We have too completely changed our intellectual horizon." Some recent words of Prof. Wm. James may serve as a warning: "The theological machinery that spoke so livingly to our ancestors, with its finite age of the

[1] *History of England*, by G. M. Trevelyan, p. 51.

world, its creation out of nothing, its judicial morality and eschatology, its relish for rewards and punishments, its treatment of God as an external contriver and 'intelligent and moral governor,' sounds as odd to most of us as if it were some outlandish, savage religion" (*A Pluralistic Universe*, p. 29).[1]

But we must never forget that the mental and spiritual development of man is a very gradual process, and that individuals are at innumerable and very distantly separated stages of spiritual growth. There are millions of souls to-day who find help and support in the doctrinal and sacramental structure which has been gradually built up round the person of an Atoner and Mediator, whom they adore as divine as well as human, and delight to think of as "our Lord and Saviour Jesus Christ," "the Way, the Truth, and the Life," who will bring them into union with the Father. For while "broader and more learned minds are always cramped by the thought of God as a Person, for Personality limits to place and time, childlike, untrained minds say that God is a personal Being." The statement that God is Principle chills them, and in terror they cry out: "They have taken away my Lord, and I know not where they have laid Him!"[2]

But in whatever form, simple or complicated,

[1] In "Jesus or Christ?", the *Hibbert Journal Supp.*, p. 58.
[2] H. Emilie Cady's *Lessons in Truth*, chap. i. p. 13.

religion is accepted it must make the inculcation of morality its chief object, and there is only one thing which can be the starting-point and the kernel of it. That thing is the religion of love as taught by Jesus. It is true that, as theologians have recently discovered, the Prophet of Nazareth taught it with a background, or world-view (Welt-anschauung), which is to us to-day almost unintelligible, but his religion can be separated from that, and it is enshrined as a "possession for ever" for mankind in the Synoptic Gospels.

That religion of love gives the rule and the motive power of the new form of thought, half-science, half-religion, which we know as Spiritualism, and which to many seekers after truth and spiritual power, both simple and learned, has come as what Conan Doyle called it: "A New Revelation." It has not been as much as that to the writer, who was brought up a High Churchman and has never for a moment doubted the fact of survival, but he has benefited by it very much, mentally and spiritually, and to a small extent, as it happens, physically.

The Seven Principles of Spiritualism as at present stated are:

1. The Fatherhood of God.
2. The Brotherhood of Man.
3. The Communion of Spirits and the Ministry of Angels.
4. The continuous existence of the human soul.
5. Personal Responsibility.

6. Compensation and Retribution hereafter for all the good deeds and all the evil deeds done on earth.
7. Eternal Progress open to every human soul.

They include, surely, little or nothing that is positively inconsistent with Christianity, but they stand in negative opposition to it in that they omit not only creeds and sacraments with the institutions necessary for their preservation and administration, but also the fundamental doctrines of the Incarnation and the Atonement. The writer ventures to offer the following as a supplement to them:—

God is a power not ourselves which makes for righteousness,[1]
in whom Justice and Love are inseparable
like the concave and the convex of a curve,
because He works out His divine design by moral laws which execute themselves automatically,
giving compensation for good, and retribution for evil done,
perfectly in the spirit world, but imperfectly in this,
because there are so few souls which are sufficiently attuned to willing compliance with His laws.

After the Reunion of the three Methodist churches in September 1932 the President of the new church, the Rev. T. Scott Lidgett, said in his first presidential address, "Now is the time to revive perfect love. . . . We have to-day a magnificent opportunity, for rulers, statesmen, and economists, having tried all

[1] Matthew Arnold's definition.

they can to meet the crying needs of the age, are coming to a common recognition that only a great spiritual revival can suffice to carry mankind through the tremendous difficulties which beset civilisation throughout the world."

Christianity has been trying for nineteen centuries to train mankind to put spiritual values above material ones. It has done much good, but has been the cause of much evil, and it has been unable to prevent much more. Let anyone who disputes this contemplate the world to-day. We see nearly all the Christian nations armed to the teeth—whether they can afford it or not!—and in constant fear of the "war to end war" being soon followed by a still more terrible one. Nationalism is rampant under the guise of patriotism (!), because the whole social and economic system is based upon class distinctions, competition, and hardly mitigated selfishness and greed. Serious thought is confined to a small minority. And the situation is made worse by the unprecedented facilities for amusement, and the influence of a press, much of which cares for little but increasing its profits by pandering to the shallow and often degraded tastes of the bulk of its readers.

During the last hundred years, however, two new movements have sprung into existence which are leading a wiser minority in the right direction. The first of these is Socialism, which preaches the Brotherhood of Man, co-operation instead of competition, and puts the interests of society above the profit or the interest of the individual. The other is Spiritualism, which by proving the fact of our future existence, and teaching us its laws and its conditions, makes it clear that the only way to ensure our happiness in the spirit world is to promote the welfare and happiness of others in this one by practising the Golden Rule, and working with all one's might to realise the Brotherhood of Man.

Now Socialism is at bottom science and common sense applied to society with the animating motive of "Reverence for Life." That means acknowledging that even the bottom dog has a right to his share of all the advantages that society, if organised on right principles, is now in a position to provide for all its members. And the recognition of the supreme value of human life means an admission that spiritual, not material values, are the ultimate standard of judgment, and that, too, in politics and industry as well as in other and personal matters.

Spiritualism also must be recognised universally as including a "psychic" science, though, of course, that science is a very young one. Investigation of its phenomena only began about 1850, but there are now scores of volumes accessible to any inquirer who wishes to make sure of his ground before accepting it. All its phenomena, messages from discarnate spirits included, have been proved to be, when the conditions are right, perceptible to our bodily senses, and that under circumstances which preclude any suspicion of fraud. We are assured by psychic science that many of the phenomena have their origin in a spirit world normally invisible to us, yet interpenetrating our world, so that whether we believe it and like it or not, we are throughout life "compassed about by a great cloud of witnesses" (Heb. xii. 1). Is that any harder to believe than what astronomy calls on us to accept as fact, viz. that outside our solar system, and far beyond the reach of our eyes, there are millions of heavenly bodies in various stages of evolution, some of them being quite possibly the home of rational creatures like ourselves, but perhaps far more highly developed than we are?

In both these worlds Divine Law—physical, moral, and spiritual—reigns supreme, except so far as it is ignored, defied, and broken by the "unruly wills and affections" of our poor undeveloped human selves.

But the arch of human thought is nearing completion, and as it grows human progress will become easier and more rapid. The pier of Science remains unchanged, like granite; but the other pier, that of non-scientific, humanistic, religious thought, constructed to all appearance of mouldable concrete, has now been discovered to be reinforced by the iron of science. Religion has always looked up to, and depended on, an invisible world of spiritual life. Psychic science has now *proved* that invisible world to exist, and to be a part of what we have to accept as our "real" world as truly as is the physical, material world which we all accept as "real" to us without demanding any proof that it is so.

Hence, as time goes on, the need for faith, except in the sense of loyalty, will grow less and less.

"Faith will vanish into sight," except so long as it remains still a necessity for some people to enable them to believe in the existence of the unseen world, or to help them in appropriating the moral power it offers.

"Hope be emptied in delight" at once for those who deserve it, and in time even for those whose earthly lives condemn them to varying periods of corrective discipline in the lower circles of the etheric spheres.

"Love, even here, will shine more bright," because, having left behind us, as one of the naïve ideas belonging to the childhood of the race, the belief that a sudden acceptance of the atoning power of a Saviour's death can nullify the effects of a life of selfishness or crime, we shall see clearly and feel irresistibly that love provides, even here, the only way in which we can avoid sin or atone for it, so as to show ourselves worthy threads in the great Divine Design, and assure ourselves of a happy, "heavenly" future.

# BIBLIOGRAPHY

### BOOKS QUOTED

*The Quest of the Historical Jesus.* Dr Albert Schweitzer. A. & C. Black. German, 1906; English, 1910.

*Civilisation and Ethics.* Dr Schweitzer. A. & C. Black. 2nd Edition. 1929.

*The Mysticism of Paul the Apostle.* Dr Schweitzer. A. & C. Black. 1931.

*Albert Schweitzer: My Life and Thought.* G. Allen and Unwin. 1933.

*Miracles and Modern Spiritualism.* Dr A. R. Wallace. 1872.

*The Life of St Francis of Assisi.* Paul Sabatier. Hodder & Stoughton. 1908.

*The Student's Old Testament.* Prof. Kent. 5 vols. Hodder & Stoughton. 1904-7.

*Old and New Conceptions of the Old Testament.* Philip Wicksteed. No. 11 of the M'Quaker Trust Lectures. Ph. Green, Essex Street, Strand. 1897. 1d.

*Personal Religion in Egypt before Christianity.* Prof. Sir Flinders Petrie. Harper's Library of Living Thought. 1912.

*Commentary on the Bible.* Dr Peake. Jack. 1920.

*Between the Old and New Testaments.* Canon R. H. Charles. Home University Library. Seventh Edition. 1929.

*Rabbi, Messiah, Martyr.* Herbert Rix. Ph. Green, Essex Street. 1907.

*Human Personality.* F. W. H. Myers. Longmans. 1906. Abridged Edition. 1907.

*Varieties of Religious Experience.* Prof. W. James. Longmans. 1902. 14th Impression, 1907.
*The Religious Teachings of Jesus.* C. G. Montefiore. Macmillan. 1910.
"Jesus or Christ?", *Hibbert Journal Supplement.* Various Writers. Williams and Norgate. 1909.
*Christ, Yesterday and To-day.* G. B. Jeffery, F.R.S. G. Allen and Unwin. 1934.
*On the Edge of the Etheric.* J. A. Findlay. Rider. 1931.
*Spirit Teachings.* Stainton Moses (M.A.Oxon.). London Spiritual Alliance. 1883. Tenth Edition. 1924.
*Your Infinite Possibilities.* Marg. V. Underhill. Rider. 1931.
*Towards the Stars.* H. Dennis Bradley. T. Werner Laurie. 1924.
*Talks with Friends of Bench and Bar.* By a Retired Public Servant through trance mediumship. J. M. Watkins, Cecil Court, Charing Cross Road. 1931.
*History of England.* Prof. G. M. Trevelyan. Longmans. 1927. 7th Impression, 1929.
*Lessons in Truth.* H. Emilie Cady. T. L. Fowler.

## Books Helpful

*Paul and his Interpreters.* Dr Schweitzer. A. & C. Black. 1912.
*Christianity and the Religions of the World.* Dr Schweitzer. G. Allen and Unwin. 3s. 6d.
*Life beyond Death with Evidence.* Rev. H. Drayton Thomas. Collins. 3s. 6d.

# INDEX

Abraham, 28, 30.
Adonai, 50.
Anglo-Saxon Religion, 134.
Apocalyptic Books, 9, 17, 34, 47, 54, 114.
Article VI, 26
Astruc, Jean, 35.
Atonement, 112 f., 115, 123, 128.

Baal, 50.
Baptism, 84, 90, 117.
Barnes, Bishop, 95.
Betrayal, The, 76.
Bible, The, 8, 24, 27.
Bible-worship, 23, 45.
British-Israel theory, 45, 92.

Cady, Mrs, 126.
Cæsarea Philippi, 70, 73 note.
Carpenter, Dr J. E., 97
Chemosh, 50.
Chosen People, 92.
Christ, 44, 85, 97, 98, 101, 103, 113, 125.
"Christ" (The title), 51, 81, 85, 94, 97, 114.
Christianity, 55 f., 111, 133, 135, 139.
Chronicles, Book of, 38.
Copernicus, 14.
Creeds, 25, 53, 99.
"Churchianity," 117.

Dagon, 50.
Daniel, Book of, 40, 54.
Darwin, Charles, 14.
David, 31, 38.
Death, 22, 111, 117 f., 126.
Deborah, 37.
Deuteronomy, 36.
Dogma in History, 65, 68, 71, 75.
Drummond, Dr, 95.

Elias, 68, 73.
Elohim, 35, 49.
Emmaus, Journey to, 104.
Enoch, Book of, 34.
Eschatology, 54, 84, 114.
Ether, 109 f.
Eucharist, 71, note, 117.
Exile, The, 30.
Ezra, 10.

Fairbairn, Principal, 95.
Feeding of the 5000, 69.
Fourth Gospel, The, 43 f., 52, 97.
Fox Sisters, The, 15, 22.
Friends, The, 101.

Gardner, Prof. Percy, 135.
God, 26, 30, 50, 90, 123, 124.

Heath, Prof. A. E., 132.
Hell, 23, 118.
Henotheism, 27, 92.
Hermetic Literature, 43.
*Hibbert Journal*, 95.
Higher Criticism, 31-4.
History, 47.

Inspiration, 29, 124.

James, Prof. Wm., 120, 128.
Jehovah, 49.
Jesus, 16, 53, 74 f., 101, 104, 130.
Job, Book of, 41.
John the Baptist, 68, 73.
Judaisers, 83, 91-3.
Judaism, 9, 53, 83.
Judas, 77.
Judges, 28, 30 f., 37.
Judgment, Day of, 116.
Justification by Faith, 91.

KINGDOM OF HEAVEN (the Messianic), 17, 53 f., 89.

LAW, The, 82-4, 91.
Liberal Theology, 56.
Life in the Beyond, 22, 126, 128.
Life in Christ, 89.
"Life" (Mrs Barbauld's poem), 117.
Lodge, Sir Oliver, 108.
Logos, The, 43, 97.
"LORD, The," 49.
Lord's Prayer, The, 72.
Love, Religion of, 119, 130 f.

MACCABEES, The, 40.
Malachi, 73.
Man's Origin, 122.
Mary, The Virgin, 99, 111.
Mediums, 23, 110.
Messages, 120-130.
Messiah, The, 17 f., 47, 51, 61, 73, 84-6, 88, 106.
Messiah-to-be, 66, 69, 104.
Messiah, Birthpangs of the, 17.
Messianic Secret, 20, 66, 68, 74.
Miracles, 19.
Mission of the XII, 68, 72.
Mistranslations, 49-51.
Modernism, 21.
Moloch, 50.
Monotheism, 27, 51.
Montefiore, C. G., 83.
Moses, 34.
Myers, F. W. H., 78.
Mysticism, 18.

NEW AGE, The, 17, 84, 89, 96.
Nicæa, 25.
Nicene Creed, 58, 111 f.
Nonentities!, 129.

OLD TESTAMENT HISTORY, 28, 36.
Olympian Theology, 12.

PAUL, St, 16, 48, 79-81, 105, 113.
his Theology, 82-90, 92 f., 98, 114.

Pentateuch, The, 27, 34.
Peter, St, 70, 76, 105.
Physics, 109.
Predestination, 92 f.
Priestly Code (P.C.), 36, 39.
Progress, 132.
Prophets, The Old Testament, 29, 39, 41, 50.
Psalms, Book of, 41.
Psychic power of Jesus, 104.
Ptolemy, the Astronomer, 14
Purgatory, 19.

*Quest of the Historical Jesus,* 64.

*Rabbi, Prophet, Martyr,* 57-64.
Ransom for many, 75, 113 note.
Redemption, Paul's Doctrine of, 86-88.
Religion, 123, 124, 141.
Religions, Origin of, 111.
Resurrection, 20, 78.
"Revelation, The" (Apocalypse), 44.
Richet, Prof., 22, 108.
Rix, Herbert, 57.

SABATIER, Paul, 19.
Salvation, 115, 128.
Schweitzer, Dr Albert, 9, 11, 55, 65, 100, 104, 130.
Science, Modern, 21, 46, 109, 141.
Sin, 87 f.
Socialism, 139 f.
Solomon, The Psalms of, 34.
Spiritualism, 15, 22, 115, 119, 139 f.
  Principles of, 115, 137.
  and Christianity, 55 f.
Stainton Moses, 115.
Supper, The Last, 69 f.

TEMPLE OF SOLOMON, The, 29.
Temptation, 72, 76.
Thales, 13, 112.
Transfiguration, 73 f., 104.

Translations, 49.
Trinity, Doctrine of the, 52.
Triumphal Entry, 76.
Twelve, Mission of the, 67-9.

WALLACE, Dr A. R., 15, 133.
Westcott, Bishop, 95.

*Wonderful Century, The*, 133.
"Word" or "Wisdom" of God, 43.
World-view, 11, 18, 131, 137.

YAHWEH, 26, 29, 35, 37, 49 f., 92.

For Product Safety Concerns and Information please contact our EU representative GPSR@taylorandfrancis.com
Taylor & Francis Verlag GmbH, Kaufingerstraße 24, 80331 München, Germany

www.ingramcontent.com/pod-product-compliance
Lightning Source LLC
Chambersburg PA
CBHW070837020526
44114CB00041B/1951